The Age of the Archangel Michael

Books by Emil Bock

Genesis

Moses

Kings and Prophets

Caesars and Apostles

The Childhood of Jesus

The Three Years

Saint Paul

The Apocalypse of Saint John

Studies in the Gospels: Volume 1

Studies in the Gospels: Volume 2

The Age of the Archangel Michael

The Life and Times of Rudolf Steiner

The Age of the Archangel Michael

Reflections on the True Spirit of Our Time

EMIL BOCK

Translated by Cynthia Hindes

Cover image: *Archangel Michael* by Liane Collot d'Herbois used with kind permission of Emerald Foundation, The Hague, Netherlands

First published in German as *Im michaelischen Zeitalter* by Verlag Urachhaus, Stuttgart in 1948
This translation is based on the third revised and expanded edition published in 2003

First published in English by Floris Books, Edinburgh in 2026
© 2023 Verlag Freies Geistesleben & Urachhaus GmbH
English version © 2026 Floris Books

All rights reserved. No part of this publication may be reproduced without the prior permission of Floris Books, Edinburgh
www.florisbooks.co.uk

  Also available as an eBook

Authorised EU Representative: Easy Access System Europe, Mustamae tee 50, 10621 Tallinn, Estonia gpsr.requests@easproject.com
British Library CIP data available
ISBN 978-178250-991-2

Contents

Foreword by Tom Ravetz   7

1. Courage in Thinking *(1923)*   11
2. In the Age of Michael *(1937)*   18
3. Between Two Michael Ages *(1938)*   27
4. Christian Ideals in the Age of Michael *(1940)*   43
5. The Michael Age in Autumn *(1945)*   64
6. The Confrontation with Evil *(1947)*   73
7. Europe's Inspiring Spirit *(1947)*   86
8. The World Situation and the True Spirit of the Times *(1949)*   92
9. The Millennium *(1950)*   103
10. The Age of Light *(1953)*   113
11. Michael and the New Coming of Christ *(1953)*   116
12. Christians and the Conscience of the Times *(1955)*   123
13. Progressive Christianity *(1955)*   129
14. Michael's Transformations *(1948)*   139
15. Michael, the Prince of Progress *(1956)*   143
16. Christ and Michael *(1956)*   149
17. The Spirit of Michael: Celebrating Transformation *(1957)*   156

Notes   161
Bibliography   163

Foreword

These essays, written between 1923 and 1957, arose out of the addresses and lectures that Emil Bock gave almost yearly on the subject of the age of the Archangel Michael. They reflect his earnest engagement with two great streams: an inner stream related to Christian theology, whose renewal through the insights and anthroposophical research of Rudolf Steiner he sought to serve, and an outer stream concerned with contemporary culture, society and technological progress.

I first read this book in German more than thirty years ago, at a time when the world still seemed shaped by many of the events Bock discusses here: the aftermath of the First World War, the rising storm of Nazism, the geopolitical divisions of East and West, and the breakthrough into the subatomic realm. Approaching it again now, I wondered if Bock's reflections would remain relevant for readers who stand at a distance from those events, separated by new catastrophes and revolutions. Too often, even with the most esteemed authors, the passage of time and the gulf in language and thought that inevitably arises makes their insights inaccessible or seem outdated.

Instead, I found myself confronted page after page by insights that spoke with fresh clarity, filled with both courage and understanding. In the very first essay Bock asks:

> How do we become co-champions with Michael? By making our thinking into a real questioning and struggle for the spirit, fired by true courage.

Thinking and courage in the service of the Archangel Michael form a thread that runs throughout the book. They give it the quality of a workbook for our own tasks today, guiding us both in deepening our knowledge of the spiritual world and in engaging with unfolding world events with compassion and discernment. Many people are shocked by the instability of our present age, where much that we thought was settled and established, especially in the liberal democracies, has been thrown into turmoil. In this we may be closer to Bock's world now than we were even twenty years ago, and what he wrote of his own time could easily have been penned for us:

> In all of world history, there has probably never been an age whose destiny has been as difficult to understand as the one in which we are now living. Countless lives have come to a violent end, and entire streams of historical development that had stood secure for millennia have been destroyed. If we only look at the earthly realities, we really cannot understand the meaning of our time. We are faced with irresolvable riddles.

Bock makes the task clear: we must look beyond the surface of events to the forces working behind and through them. Only in this way can we 'grasp the essential meaning and purpose' of our time.

The figure to whom Bock continually points is, of course, the Archangel Michael. Drawing on biblical and mystical tradition, and the insights of Rudolf Steiner, he paints the picture of the guardian spirit of our age:

> Michael tirelessly ploughs the field of humanity so that the spiritual seed he scatters in such abundance can flourish. He rattles and shakes humanity; our awakening to the spirit is more important to him than our outward well-being. Much of the old must fall away so that the new can emerge.

Through Bock's eyes we learn to perceive our modern world as Michael sees it, and we realise that the great storms that surround us temporarily mask a much greater light that even now is shining in from supersensible spheres. This reordering of vision changes our priorities. We begin to recognise how much of our distress at change arises from our attachment to our own comfort and our reluctance to face up to what the world needs from us if it is to progress further.

Bock's comments on technology, too, help us find a healthy stance: one that neither shuns it nor surrenders to it, but helps us to engage properly with it. His insights also remind us that Michael's connection to the cosmic intelligence has relevance for our debates on so-called artificial intelligence today.

Above all, Bock directs our gaze to the true battle of our time: the battle of Michael with the dragon and humanity's confrontation with evil. Bock interprets our age as the continuation of the 'war in heaven' described in Revelation, Chapter 12. Yet he also stresses the resources we are given, above all through the life of devotion:

> Today, we must find the path to a kind of devoutness that modern humans can once again cultivate honestly. It is the religion of resting in the golden middle, in the sphere of Christ, which is also the sphere of Michael. Although it seems paradoxical, cultivating peace is also the most effective way of fighting evil ... From a soul filled with peace, which we gain through devotion and piety in the sacramental sense, a new morality emerges.

The range of these essays is wide, and I have only touched on a few themes here. I hope this brief introduction will encourage you to engage more deeply with Bock's vision. His final words remain as consoling for us as for his first readers:

> And so we want to look forward with great joyful expectation to what the future holds. The future will undoubtedly bring many horrors, but if we listen to Michael's apocalyptic language, it will also bring us a new closeness to Christ if only we venture out onto the stormy sea of change in this new age of Michael.

Tom Ravetz
Lenker of The Christian Community
in Great Britain and Ireland
2025

1
Courage in Thinking
(1923)

A Catholic theology professor was once asked in his seminar how the individual priest should deal with the fact that the church contradicts the doctrine of evolution. The professor replied: 'If Rome condemns this or that doctrine, it does not mean that it is wrong.'

The questioner and his fellow students were satisfied with this answer and instantly relieved of their doubts. Only one young Protestant student who was present covered his face in dismay. He did not understand the professor, much less those who were satisfied with his answer. He found himself facing an utterly alien world.

Such an incident reveals the helpless, unthinking attitude of institutional Christianity in the face of advancing human thought.

Since Copernicus and Galileo, the Catholic Church has seen in the emerging scientific thinking a ravening wolf that must be held back in the forecourt of the temple so that it does not enter the inner sanctum. The Church did not criticise natural science for containing no truth at all – indeed, she even singled out the sharpest thinkers from the ranks of her own priesthood as learned representatives of natural science – but for being dangerous. This ultimately was the charge against Galileo, not for teaching what was untrue.

Protestantism on the other hand, which emerged around the same time, failed to grasp the true nature of the modern scientific thinking growing up alongside it. Unsuspectingly, it let the wolf into its sanctuary dressed in the sheep's clothing of truth. Certainly, the feeling of apprehension that led, and continues to lead, the deliberate and planned defence of the Catholic Church repeatedly arose in Protestantism. Wherever something like the Catholic attitude towards scientific thinking asserted itself in Protestant ranks, people spoke of the need to separate faith and knowledge for the sake of faith. But this response was of a more instinctive and unquestioning character. It could not prevent the wolf from finding its way into the theological field where intellectual, materialistic thinking directed its unfathomed destructive power at the Holy Scriptures. In the end, the Bible was stolen out from under people without them even realising it.

Catholicism's temple still towers imposingly high. But for all its power, it is an old man. Along with the wolf, it has also kept away a rejuvenating, progressive element. The temple owes its continued outdated existence to the 'No' that stems from fear of the wolf. After all, a dominant ruler can also act out of fear.

The temple that Protestantism could have built around its Holy of Holies remained unbuilt. Although there were people in the Protestant camp who maintained their warm, believing hearts, the wolf knew how to prevent the building of the temple. It allowed understanding of the community-building power of the sacraments to die, and when people demanded that there should be no limit to critical thinking regarding the Bible, they believed they were serving the truth. In reality, they allowed a thinking that had become ungodly to enter the realm of the divine Word. The wolf has long since raided the unprotected Holy of Holies.

The warning attitude that the Catholic Church takes towards the modern seeker for truth is best symbolised by the myth of the youth of Saïs. In ancient Egypt, a young man approached the mystery temple at Saïs. The priests accepted him among their disciples, led him through all the rooms of their temple, showed him all the sacred signs and taught him the high wisdom they had received. It was only as they drew near to the Holy of Holies that they fell silent, walking wordlessly past a veiled statue. The young man demanded to know what was hidden beneath the veil, but the priests warned him that before the statue all questions must cease. The young man was not satisfied with this. He became consumed with the idea of the veiled statute and was unable to sleep. Finally, his desire to know the truth became overwhelming. In a fever he approached the statute, reached for the veil and pulled it away. Legend has it that the priests found the young man the next day, dead at the feet of the unveiled image. His soul had been too weak to bear the overwhelming power of the divine image.

The Catholic Church still treats the modern thinker who

1. COURAGE IN THINKING

searches for the divine like the priests did the disciple of Saïs thousands of years ago. It acts as if human beings had not progressed in all that time, and as if that high divine being had not come to earth to give strength and freedom to human souls.

People who have awakened to the demands of the present age ask questions like the youth of Saïs. With the awakening of the questioning mind and the courage to ask questions, the story of the youth of Saïs was replaced by another: that of Parsifal and the search for the Holy Grail.

Parsifal wandered through the world a dreaming fool, and though he was frequently amazed by what he saw, he never questioned anything. He had not yet achieved that clear, wide-awake awareness that made it possible for him, out of freedom, to ask questions. Parsifal's destiny led him to the Grail castle. There, at a lavish banquet, he saw how the Grail fed the hearts and bodies of the knights, and he saw Amfortas, the Grail King, who suffered from a wound that even the Grail could not heal. Despite his amazement, Parsifal still did not question what was happening. What the youth of Saïs had not yet been allowed to do, Parsifal should have done but could not. The next day, Parsifal found himself back in the wilderness. The Grail castle had disappeared. He then had to return to the forest and endure a long period of trials, until such time as the courage to ask the right question emerged in him. Only when he finally achieved that courage was he able to re-enter the Grail castle, heal the wounded Amfortas, and become the Grail King.

Humanity has awakened. It has progressed from the time of the youth at Saïs to that in which Parsifal must enquire about the high kingship in the temple realm.

It might seem at first as if the Protestant attitude towards modern thinking is already a commitment to the Parsifal question. But in truth, it is far from an awakened deed. From the very beginning, it was swept along by the scientific way of thinking, which had emerged shortly before through a push occurring in the general development of consciousness. We can compare it to a person who wakes in the morning feeling well rested: the process is a natural one and not the result of a courageous, voluntary self-awakening.

It is, therefore, understandable that the new way of thinking that Protestantism went along with remained mere head thinking. It did not take hold of the whole human being because it did not come from an awakened heart. Following a trend of the times, human beings began to think coherent thoughts about the visible world. A rich, artfully crafted scientific and ideological system subsequently emerged, but it was pale and bloodless. The heart's awakening did not follow the head's awakening. Humanity's inner nature, which alone could have given life and full reality to the head's thoughts, became, if anything, duller and more unconscious.

This signalled the beginning of a dangerous split in human souls. With their newly given powers of thought, human beings quickly took possession of the sensory world, and their more active mental life gave them a wealth of new sensory impressions. But the deeper, more unconscious layers of their being responded with a flood of unrecognised and unrefined desires and urges. The more childlike naivety and innocence faded away, the more consciousness, filled as it was with earthly perceptions and abstract thoughts, was confronted with the unawakened unconscious, which itself was filled with the fire of sensuality.

Without wanting to, and without knowing it, human beings sent up into their thoughts everything that was obscure and unclear from the depths of their unconscious. Thoughts and words veiled what was instinctive in humanity; cleverness became an instrument of egotism. We see the consequences of this today in our everyday life: politics, science, even theology, are filled with 'buzzwords'. Despite all its logical correctness, thinking is weakened and distorted by the unrefined unconscious. Because it is not taken up by a courageous and deliberately cultivated inner strength, it does not rise above the world of the outer senses, and not having risen to the world of the spirit, it no longer understands the world of the senses either. It spreads a densely woven web of deception over everything, considering the things of the world to be nothing but dead matter. Materialism of thought is an error because it stems from human iniquity. The marriage between what is unrefined and instinctual and the head's abstract concepts gives rise to a world of ghosts, which human beings ultimately help to make visible.

1. COURAGE IN THINKING

According to ancient Germanic mythology, Fenris Wolf was born from Loki (Lucifer), the tempter who dwells in the raging flames. If human beings leave their Luciferic instinctual drives untransformed, their own thoughts attack them from the outside world like ravening wolves. The fear that causes Catholicism to seal off the temple against thinking is the fear of the wolf, which human beings of the present are constantly calling into being. The affirmation of thinking in Protestantism is an unsuspecting co-birthing of the wolf as long as that thinking is not elevated by a conscious and constantly renewed courageous act of transformation and awakening. Neither Catholicism nor Protestantism does anything to ask the Parsifal question and attain its promised Grail kingship; thought is not Christianised and redeemed, and neither resists the beast that rises from the abyss of our inner being, the dragon that gives birth to the wolf in the field of human thought.

The dragon and the wolf are facts of our present spiritual existence. No matter where we turn, we cannot escape them. Either our last sanctuaries fall victim to them, and with them, our souls, or we take up the fight against them. From which side will we receive help and strength for the battle?

When the age of the new intellectual consciousness dawned, the image of Parsifal was placed before human souls as a sign that the time of the veiled image of Saïs had expired. Human beings have learnt to think intellectually; they have summoned the spirits like the sorcerer's apprentice in Goethe's poem. But now the spirits are storming us and we cannot escape them. The time has come for Parsifal to be joined by another figure, that of Michael, the archangel of courage, who is the countenance of Christ:

> Then war broke out in heaven. Michael and his angels fought against the dragon, and the dragon, and his angels fought back. But he was not strong enough, and they lost their place in heaven. The great dragon was hurled down – that ancient serpent called the devil, or Satan, who leads the whole world astray. He was hurled to the earth, and his angels with him. (Rev. 12:7–10)

How do we become co-champions with Michael? By making our thinking into a real questioning and struggle for the spirit, fired by true courage. If we ask the Parsifal question with humility and courage, we break the spell that has been placed upon the world into which we gaze. Instead of the dark, dragon-like life of instincts and drives, our love, goodwill and spiritual courage become the soul of our thoughts. Our active love for the spirit is the spear of light with which we slay the dragon within us. Into the world of our thoughts, which we have allowed to become a ravening wolf, and into the world of the senses, which we endeavour to comprehend through our thoughts, we can carry the spirit won through courage and love when we fight in the army of Michael.

It is no longer acceptable for us to ward off the wolf of the critical mind at the threshold of the sanctuary after we have called it into being. But it is also no longer acceptable simply to let it rage. We must approach it with courage and transform it. When we do this, we redeem it in our own thinking and the sensory world that we have populated with ghosts. Thinking must be given a courageous and conscious share in the sanctuary of inwardness, but for this to happen it must be changed from within. Heart and head must be educated to work together in a way of thinking fuelled by the heart and flowing with love. Such thinking is capable of understanding and recognising not only the sense-perceptible world but also the supersensible world and can, therefore, only then find the full truth about the world around us.

St Francis of Assisi once came to the village of Gubbio in the northeastern part of Italy. The village was beset by a monstrous wolf that ate not only animals but also people. St Francis went to confront the ferocious animal, bravely calling out, 'Come here, brother wolf.' The wolf came, meekly as a lamb, and lay quietly at St Francis' feet. From that hour onwards, the wolf lived peacefully in the village without harming anyone. This legend gives us a prophetic picture of the Michaelic deed that must be done to human thinking on a large scale.

In the yearly cycle, Michaelmas begins on the threshold of autumn, when we enter the colder, darker season. Thus, the Michaelic spiritual courage, through which the heart awakens to become an organ of perception, allows us to carry light and warmth into the cold winter of merely intellectual thinking. Just before Michaelmas, the sun enters the sign of Libra. The heart's love, now awakened to spiritual courage, holds the balance between the unconscious, instinct-filled abyss of our being and the thoughts of our heads.

Living Michaelically means wedding the inner and the outer through courageous strength of heart. Redeemed thinking is the beginning of the Michaelic life. Those who allow love to flow up from the depths of their inner being into their thoughts and sense perceptions no longer name the things and beings of the world with learned words. Instead, they greet them as brothers and sisters. Their thinking becomes a greeting and a naming out of the rediscovered divine mission of creation (Gen. 2:19).

Michaelic thinking also brings us higher truth and wisdom through the world of the senses. It becomes Michael's spear with which he can pierce the ghostly veil woven by the dragon's power. Through the heart's courage, thinking transforms into seeing. In this seeing, we become, 'knowing out of feeling', and like Parsifal, we become 'knowing out of compassion'. The light-spear of beholding thought divides the curtain of material existence, and the spiritual realm where Michael serves Christ among his angels opens up before us.

Ultimately, unredeemed thinking, however brilliant it may be, can only lead to talk of the decline of the West. But if at least some people awaken their souls to Michaelic thinking and seeing amid the dire challenges of our time, then, instead of this deterioration, we will be able to speak of the rise of a new Christ-revelation.

2

In the Age of Michael
(1937)

Whoever wants to stand firmly within their time and grasp its essential meaning and purpose cannot be content merely with observing what is happening around them. They must endeavour to penetrate to the divine intentions from which the events of their era flow. They must learn to recognise where the hands of the inner World Clock stand.

In 1508, the Rosicrucian Abbot of Sponheim, Johannes von Trithemius, wrote a short treatise that can serve as an important aid in every age for achieving such an inner orientation. The essential contents of this treatise were later confirmed by Rudolf Steiner.[1]

According to the abbot, periods in history are guided by one of seven archangels, who rise repeatedly to the rank of time spirit to become the inspiring spirit of the age. Each period, or regency, lasts for about as many years as there are days in the year. By looking up to the archangel who guides each age, people living on earth can gain insight into the events of their time and God's intention for it.

Since 1879 we have been living in an age of Michael, the archangel of the sun, who took over the stewardship of world history from Gabriel, the archangel of the moon. What is the essence of a Michael age? If we look at that period in history when the Archangel Michael last assumed rulership of the age, we can gain insights into our own time. The previous Michael age ran from the seventh to the third century BC, and almost immediately we recognise three outstanding features of that historically significant epoch.

The first is that hardly any other age had such an immeasurable wealth of enlightened spiritual leaders as that one. Wherever we look in the world, we marvel at the rich, illustrious assembly of great spirits that appear almost simultaneously. Among them are the Old Testament prophets, from Isaiah, Jeremiah, Ezekiel,

2. IN THE AGE OF MICHAEL

Daniel and Jonah to Ezra and Nehemia. Living and working alongside them were the great philosophers of Greece, from Heraclitus and Pythagoras to Socrates, Plato and Aristotle. In their still God-given thoughts, Western thought was born. The thinkers are joined by artists such as the sculptors Phidias and Praxiteles, and the playwrights Aeschylus, Sophocles and Euripides. Countless names could be mentioned to indicate Greece's part in this great gathering of spirits.

This was also the time, over in India, of Gautama Buddha, the Enlightened One. Quietly, yet more powerfully than any other teacher of humanity of historical times, he planted in souls the longing for the supersensible. The historical Zarathustra, the great teacher of the Persians, was also a son of the previous Michael age. He renewed the ancient Zoroastrian solar wisdom, which we find in the marvellous sayings of the Gathas in the Zend-Avesta. Looking further east, we encounter the luminous multitude of the Chinese sages: the mystic Lao Tzu and the moral teacher Confucius were contemporaries of the Israelite prophets and Greek philosophers.

This abundance of lofty spirits on earth is a mystery that only becomes clear when we see the Archangel Michael as the inspiring spirit of the age at the head of humanity. He endeavours with all his power to let rays of spiritual light penetrate those souls who are receptive to it, and his messengers are the many great spirits who appear on earth. The rich, multifaceted spiritual life that blossomed everywhere in humanity in such marvellous simultaneity stemmed from Michael's inspiration.

The second characteristic of that Michael age is closely related to the first: great storms roar over humanity and nations rise up against nations. Michael's rulership is by no means an epoch of peace and calm. The last time Michael's reign dawned, the prophet Isaiah spoke to his people as the Assyrian army approached and demolished ten of the twelve tribes of Israel. A tiny country under constant threat became the scene of a rich prophetic, spiritual culture until that remnant was also crushed. In the homelessness of the later Babylonian captivity, the prophetic spiritual life reached its most sublime peaks. But we only realise the dynamics of the Michael age when we take a broader view the great upheavals going on in the world at the time.

During that time, the Assyrians built a world empire with mighty cities as symbols of their power. But it lasted less than a hundred years. By then, it had already been overthrown by the Babylonians, whose ruler, Nebuchadnezzar, likewise commemorated his reign with an immeasurable passion for building. Once again, however, this far-reaching empire lasted only a short time. The armies of Cyrus the Great of Persia – who we can view as a messenger of the Michaelic spirit of the age – put an end to it. Following this, the waves of Persian power surged from the newly established Achaemenid Empire to the shores of Europe. The small nation of the Greeks heroically turned back the Persian conquest of the continent in the Persian Wars. Finally, before the end of the Michael period, the rapid miracle of Alexander the Great's march east changed the world's entire political and spiritual order. In twelve years, the young Macedonian king conquered the great empires and forged a new one from them, permeating it with the still young, European spiritual element.

The stormy turbulence of the age is also a riddle that can only be solved by looking at the archangel of the sun himself. Michael tirelessly ploughs the field of humanity so that the spiritual seed he scatters in such abundance can flourish. He rattles and shakes humanity; our awakening to the spirit is more important to him than our outward well-being. Much of the old must fall away so that the new can emerge.

A third characteristic of the previous Michael age is the longing that arose, in many different places, for a divine being who would soon appear to bring about the salvation of humanity. The hope and expectation of Christ took on the most diverse forms as people across the world perceived this cosmic being drawing closer to humanity. The Old Testament prophets loudly proclaimed the coming of the Messiah. The Greek philosophers from Heraclitus to the Stoics spoke about the Logos, the creative centre of the world, as did the evangelist John. The Persian prophet Zarathustra predicted the incarnation of the high sun spirit. Even Lao Tzu, without clearly realising it, spoke of Christ in his *Tao Te Ching*, the 'Book of the Way'. In it he sought to come close to the mystery of the Logos, which he referred to with the primal word Tao.

The omnipresent shining forth of the idea of Christ or the

2. IN THE AGE OF MICHAEL

Logos was especially the result of the working of the Michaelic spirit. In the hierarchical realms, the Archangel Michael is at all times what John the Baptist would later be among humanity: a forerunner of Christ. Michael's work, especially when he rules an age, is always to prepare for a new revelation of Christ. Thus, the Michaelic centuries that preceded our era were filled with the rays of light that heralded the sunrise of the incarnation of Christ.

What features of the previous Michael age can we recognise in this new age of Michael? The second is the most obvious. Today, no one can deny that we are living in a time when storms are breaking continuously over humanity. Perhaps, in the early part of Michael's reign, the true character of the age was not yet recognisable. But the outbreak of the war in 1914 was more than the discharge of a political conflict. With the force of a cosmic catastrophe, tensions and storms erupted from the depths of existence, revealing the true dynamics of the new historical epoch. Only a superficial understanding can think that the storms have finally blown over now that the war has ended. The dynamics of world war continue to grow, even in countries that were not involved in the conflict at the time. Once again Michaelic storms are sweeping across the earth. Once again, he is at work, relentlessly shaking humanity to bring us to a spiritual awakening. The fact that we still have centuries of high tension ahead of us need not frighten us; being the son or daughter of a Michaelic era is a privilege of destiny.

The above was written two years before the outbreak of the Second World War. It was already in print in German when the meeting between Chamberlain, Daladier, Hitler and Mussolini took place in Munich on Michaelmas Day 1938. A meeting which, at the time at least, seemed surprisingly to avert the danger of war. Still, for those who were under no illusion about events, it was nothing more than a warning of the coming storm. War broke out again and escalated into an incomprehensible unleashing of hell. Even in the first stage of this new catastrophe, the degree of upheaval and destruction soon surpassed that brought about by the First World War. In the end, the debris fields and ash heaps of Central Europe's ruined cities stared up at the sky. The atomic bombs forced the conclusion of a phase of the war in the Far East, employing forces of a wholly inscrutable and yet apocalyptic nature. Simultaneously, in a terrifying signal, they illuminated once again the monstrous East–West tension that had been growing acute. It had to be recognised that the term 'Second World War' was no longer sufficient to describe what had happened. It had been more than just a war. Spiritual clashes, even spirit slaughters, had broken out. They had led to the collapse and downfall of an entire old world. It is even more apparent than after the First World War that laying down arms cannot mean that humanity has exhausted its pent-up tensions. It cannot mean overcoming the chaos that has been stirred up. No other historical period has seen such mass deaths as those caused by human beings in our time. The countless numbers of the dead stand as stern testament and warning to the serious nature of our time.

But the Michaelic power does not plough the field of earth with trials without then sowing the seeds of the spirit in the richest abundance. Our time will not be without its inspired spiritual leaders, just as the previous Michael age had them. It will only depend on whether the archangel's human messengers are recognised. The first Michael-inspired pioneer of the spirit has already delivered his comprehensive message – Rudolf Steiner. Certainly in the times ahead, as Michael's reign approaches its climax, many bright stars will rise in the human firmament.

What about the third characteristic, the signs of a new revelation of Christ? Once again, through his powerful working on the souls and destinies of human beings, Michael wants to pave the way for Christ. The supersensible event that tradition describes as Christ's 'Second Coming' will become a fact, and in this Michael age it already shines into a growing number of souls. But it is precisely in the appearance of the first premonitions of this event that our time must differ fundamentally from the pre-Christian Michael age. At that time, humanity still possessed the last, fading powers of clairvoyance. By looking into the spiritual realm, those souls still capable of doing so perceived the ever-approaching presence of Christ. All those messianic prophecies were read from the spiritual facts themselves.

Today, however, the advancing part of humanity has lost the last remnant of the old spiritual vision. The most unheard-of

2. IN THE AGE OF MICHAEL

things can happen in the spiritual realm, yet souls are too coarse and too heavy to be aware of them. Thus, only hidden, disguised, unrecognised and misinterpreted signs of Christ's approach can at first penetrate the soul realm of humanity. Nevertheless, we must dare to point to such 'signs of the times'.

One of the most important tendencies reviving in souls everywhere could be described as an energetic worldliness. From the middle of the nineteenth century onwards, the mind of culture-creating humanity has focused increasingly on this world, leading to the rejection of all ideas relating to the hereafter. This has brought with it indifference and alienation, as well as a hostility not only towards the church, but towards religious life in general. It has sometimes even escalated into anger and hatred.

On the other hand, decidedly worldly-minded endeavours have taken on an almost religious character and intensity. The fervour and passion that earlier times had developed in the religious field now flowed, for example, into political life. Not only did nationalist tendencies, which had often been intertwined with religion in the past, now consciously emerge with their own religious character, but socialism and communism also became a kind of messianic religion, especially in Eastern Europe.

Among those who still retained a religious feeling, there was a widespread longing for a new piety in the here and now, for a religious experience of nature. For the most part, that search occurred outside the Christian churches, often in marked opposition to them; only rarely did it venture out within the traditional framework. The more extreme forms in which the striving for cosmic religion is clothed always disappear quickly from the scene, yet the 'here-and-now' trait that emerges in them becomes broader and more explicit. In the purely secular, and in the more ideological, anti-otherworldly tendencies, it is as if entirely different, unprecedented sparks were being struck out of the rock of this world. Is that not where the soul of our time fumbles and gropes for the spirit of the earth?

Through his resurrection and ascension, Christ has become the new Earth Spirit. Is his presence and nearness already making itself dimly felt today? Are not many of those who no longer want to have anything to do with Christianity nevertheless on the trail of Christ? Perhaps even more so than church Christians?

Properly understood, Christianity is of a cosmic nature – it is the true religion of this world. The Christian sacrament is celebrated in many places and altars at the same time, and Christ's presence is experienced everywhere. It is the fruition of the earthly omnipresence into which Christ has passed through his resurrection and ascension. The Christian sacrament is thus the silent answer to the loud cry of the age, heard in all tendencies towards worldliness that often manifest themselves in cultic forms.

Another significant sign of the times is the volitional will-character that all cultural life has taken on. At first, the increase was unremarkable. Then, after the first third of the twentieth century, it became explosive. A stormy radicalism shook off intellectualism, and academic ideals quickly lost their value. Impulses of will appeared on the scene, courageously and energetically attempting to achieve the 'completely new', the impossible. If we disregard all the overshooting of the mark and all the coarsening and demonisation, we can certainly recognise a Michaelic symptom in the new forces of will that emerged. Just as in his previous reign, especially in Greece, Michael channelled the power of thought to humanity, so, today, Michael wants to inspire and ignite human will. This also points to the approach of the new Christ-revelations, which, though initially distorted, we can see in this emerging volitional activity.

Christ's return will not simply happen 'from the outside', either in the sensory realm or solely in the supersensible. Just as Christ first revealed himself to the disciples after his resurrection and ascension in an inner way by indwelling their Whitsun-inspired souls, so will his new nearness manifest itself through the regeneration of new powers within human souls. It will be possible to speak of an inner 'return of Christ' reminiscent of the Whitsun event.

Certainly, what is stirring today, in all its all-too-earthliness, is far from bringing people closer to Christ. The expanding activities of the will are double-edged. On the one hand, Michael demands a radical attitude of soul from us, but there is also the perversion of this radicalism: demonic possession. Nevertheless, we can see the present alteration of will as the tumultuous initial state of a developmental process that only needs to be guided and correctly directed. It is necessary, however, to be alert to the

2. IN THE AGE OF MICHAEL

great dangers of the will that is surging into humanity.

Often enough these days, we observe how many seemingly typical people of will are inwardly quite weak and unstable, tending either towards intense mood swings or to a profound inner lack of independence. Their wilfulness is mainly due to them living more deeply into their physical bodies. It is wrong to forget the earthly in our spiritual endeavours and to lose the ground under our feet, but it is just as disastrous to forget the spirit in becoming more earthly and not take it into the process of incarnating. The human ego is of a spiritual nature. If people forget the spirit, they basically forget themselves. Their ego ultimately flutters powerlessly above them and can no longer intervene in their will. The danger arises that a person becomes robust in their will and, at the same time, weak in their ego.

The danger of forgetting the spiritual and rushing into merely external, albeit impressive, feats of will also applies to today's culture. One wants to achieve the 'completely new', and the conquering boldness it expresses deserves every admiration. But what is 'completely new'? When I ask myself this question, I always think of an experience that one can have on the Egyptian railways. On the long, fast journey through the sandy desert, despite the unbearable heat, all the windows and hatches must be tightly closed to prevent the fine sand from entering. To achieve the sensation of fresh air, a fan is left running in every compartment. However, the breeze that makes it easier for travellers to breathe does not consist of fresh air at all, but only of air that has long since become stale and is constantly blown around in circles. Fresh air can only come from outside the railway carriage.

It is the same in cultural life. As long as one remains limited to the earthly material sphere, even the most impressive cultural achievement can only be a repetition or a new mixture of things that have been around for a long time. The 'completely new' must be brought down to earth from heaven. It only becomes attainable when one's gaze and will encompass the spiritual realm. Ultimately, the desire to create something genuinely new must lead to the power of prayer being reincorporated into human endeavours in some form or other. What still rests in the womb of the spiritual worlds must be prayed down if it is to be brought to earthly effectiveness. The education of the soul in prayer, the cultivation of prayer (which does not need to have a specifically 'religious' form in the usual way) is the silent answer to the loud question that manifests itself in the earthquake-like appearance of wilfulness.

Where we place value on a new experience of community, we are reaching for a Christ-mystery. Our age is discovering the magic of community. The community should not only be a shelter and support for the individual but a means to greater effectiveness. And every effort to build a community is, in fact, a kind of conjuring of spirits because it creates a power greater than the sum of individual forces. There is a double-edge to this, however, when a humanity that knows nothing about spirits and wants to know nothing about them begins to conjure spirits. We have already felt a lot of this double-edgedness in the concentrations of power in our time.

Christ said, 'Where two or three gather in my name, there am I with them' (Matt. 18:20). These words illuminate and fulfil a crucial present tendency, especially concerning the 'return of Christ'. After all, this saying reveals the community's greater power compared to the individual's possibilities. At the same time, however, the low numbers 'two or three' emphasise with quiet energy an authenticity and substance that the large numbers of propagandistic statistics can never replace.

The Christian Community is aware that through its community-building endeavours, it is doing more than just benefiting its individual members. True community building is a means of summoning divine powers to help; it is ultimately a means of bringing to fruition the new coming of Christ. The community building that is taking place around our altar can, therefore, also be understood as a silent answer to a question that is loudly resounding from the phenomena of contemporary life.

3
Between Two Michael Ages
(1938)

It corresponds to the inner character of our time that, from year to year, the spiritual shocks and tremors that penetrate humanity's life as if from the depths take on more violent and powerful dimensions. It is becoming ever more apparent that we have entered a Michael age. In the end, only those who, either in feeling or in clear thought, find a relationship to the fact that progressive humanity today is under the guidance of the militant Archangel Michael will be able to master present-day problems.

The more the great questions of present-day life lay siege to us, the more we must learn to look from a higher perspective at what is happening on the earthly stage. What happens on earth happens, so to speak, on the lowest tier; down here, we have a restrictive view of events that rise far above our heads into the spiritual realm. If one takes Michael's image and name seriously, then a curtain has already been torn away before a whole world of spiritual beings.

If there is an Archangel Michael, then there is an abundance of higher spirits. Above all, among the great host of angels and archangels, there are seven time spirits. These seven spirits replace each other in turn every three and a half centuries in a cosmically regulated order. Their task is to bring humanity forward and equip it with spiritual impulses. We have often spoken of the great rhythm of the seven archangel ages, the secret archangel calendar that, from a higher sphere, provides information about earthly tensions and entanglements. One can compare this great, constantly renewing rhythm of seven with the lesser rhythm of the seven units of time we call the days of the week. We can then contrast the lesser week of seven days with the greater world week that consists of seven great archangel days. Each archangel day, however, is a whole age of about as many years as there are days in a year.

The seven days of the week are not of the same nature. Their inner differentiation was experienced more clearly in earlier times and was attributed to the differences between the seven planetary spheres. Even today, in the various European languages, we can infer their relationship to the planets from the names of the days of the week: Monday – Moon; Tuesday – Mars (French, *Mardi*); Wednesday – Mercury (French, *Mercredi*); Thursday – Jupiter (French, *Jeudi*); Friday – Venus (French, *Vendredi*); Saturday – Saturn; Sunday – Sun.

Like the days of the lesser week, the archangel days of the greater world week are also differentiated according to the various powers of the seven planetary spheres, only they progress in reverse order: Oriphiel is the archangel of Saturn, Anael the archangel of Venus, Zachariel the archangel of Jupiter, Raphael the archangel of Mercury, Samael the archangel of Mars, Gabriel the archangel of the Moon, and Michael the archangel of the Sun.

Every time Michael takes up his regency, the age takes on a character that makes it stand out from the other periods. This is similar to the day of the sun, Sunday, which also stands out from the course of the week. However, even in the lesser week, the meaning of Sunday is not really that of a leisurely day of rest and celebration. Its meaning would be better recognised and fulfilled if it were experienced as the culmination of the week and, at the same time, the beginning of a new week. The sun of Sunday should bring to light what has been achieved and accomplished during the week. Every Sunday should be the inner rounding off and sifting of a period of active and progressive development.

All the more, then, the 'Sundays' in the great archangel week, the Michael age, bear the character of an examination and decision that leads to new resolutions. Every Michael age relentlessly tests humanity for what is genuine and future oriented. An incorruptible solar force brings to light what has been achieved and accomplished in the previous two thousand years of human development. The fact that the Michael age in which we live today has such a testing and decision-making character is becoming increasingly obvious. The destinies of the times will become even more relentless and test us even more thoroughly. Everyone must gradually realise that the trial of inner courage and endurance has begun.

3. BETWEEN TWO MICHAEL AGES

In addition, the present Michael age is not only the first reign of Michael since the emergence of Christianity, but also the seventh archangel age in the Christian period because the events of Golgotha coincided with the age of Oriphiel. Christianity has been able to develop through a whole 'week' of archangels, and so the present day in particular will bring an almost palpable test of Christianity. What is not inwardly imbued with genuine Christian life, but is only a dead and extinguished form, will be blown to the winds like chaff by the storms of time.

In our previous reflection (see Chapter 2), we tried to shed light on the riddles of the present Michael age by comparing it with the previous Michael age from the seventh to the third centuries before Christ. We placed before us that historical epoch about to be born out of the gigantic upheavals of the dying ancient world. The Archangel Michael appeared as the great agitator, the ploughman of the field of humanity. But above all, he manifested himself as the mediator and herald of an immense wealth of spiritual light. In all the world's countries, great spirits appeared in astonishing simultaneity, as if in a majestic gathering of spirits, from the Israelite prophets and the Greek philosophers to Buddha and the Chinese sages. In this reflection, we will try to shed light on the present age by attempting to survey from Michael's point of view the time between these two ages. Let us dare to ask how the Archangel Michael himself found his way from his former leadership of humanity to his present one, and how he prepared himself for our present time. By posing such a question, we may perhaps also be able to approach what is specifically new about the present Michael age and, thus, what its innermost task actually is.

In the time between the two Michael epochs, two events occurred that fundamentally changed the inner landscape of humanity. The first was the Mystery of Golgotha. How did the Archangel Michael experience the Christ event and its continuing effect on humanity? We must bear in mind that there is the most intimate relationship between the Archangel Michael and the being of Christ. As the archangel of the sun, all of Michael's thoughts and endeavours are directed solely towards serving Christ, the high spirit of the sun, and preparing the way for him. Especially when Michael is working as the regent of an age, one can know that through everything he does, he is paving the way for a new emergence of Christ, a new revelation of Christ for the benefit of humanity. Thus, Michael's activity during the previous Michael age was solely aimed at preparing for Christ's coming. When the archangel sowed such manifold seeds of spiritual light in the mightily opened furrows of humanity, when he inspired the leaders of nations everywhere to become prophets and thinkers, he did so to equip human beings with the powers of thought that they would need to recognise and understand Christ when he appeared in their midst.

We now dare to put ourselves in the mind of Michael after he had relinquished the reins of history in the third century BC after Alexander the Great's death. It is easy to imagine that he was filled with the question: 'Will the light of thought I have given to humanity be sufficient so that when Christ arrives on earth, he will be recognised?' We can speak here tentatively of Michael's great suspense, which hovered over humanity in the spiritual realm like a concentrated cloud.

If we now consider how very few recognised Christ when he walked the earth in human form, how vanishingly small the circle was that had an inkling of his true nature, and how humanity as a whole took no notice of what took place in obscurity in Palestine, then we must come to the conclusion that the question in Michael's soul took on an increasingly anxious character. Very early in the history of Christian theology we see the extinction of an accurate understanding of Christ. The age of the Church Fathers also signalled the twilight of original Christian insight, the beginning of hopeless disputes about faith. What was originally living awareness solidified into ecclesiastical dogmas. Given such developments, one wonders if the Archangel Michael did not ask himself if his endeavours to equip humanity with the powers of thought had been in vain.

The second event that occurred in the time between the two Michael epochs drastically altered humanity's consciousness. That event, however, has been missed by humanity even more profoundly than the Mystery of Golgotha. We are barely conscious of it because it was a process that took place in the spiritual realm and only cast its shadow into earthly history. That is why it is difficult to describe it clearly.

3. BETWEEN TWO MICHAEL AGES

One indication is the attempt to draw a clear boundary between the Middle Ages and modern times. It is rare to find the view that a clearly defined event brought about the dawn of the modern era. We are almost always inclined to regard the divisions between antiquity, the Middle Ages and modern times as the result of systematising reason rather than an objective historical process itself. In reality, what we call 'modern times' was brought about by a dramatic event of the greatest significance. Confessional Protestant history has often tried to characterise Martin Luther's Reformation as the act that opened the door to the modern era. However, it has been rightly pointed out that the German Reformation was only one link in a great drama of European transformations that began long before that. In fact, the century before 1517 was full of many pre-Reformation activities and many momentous inventions and discoveries that completely changed the horizon of progressive development.

In 1413, the point on the horizon where the sun rises in spring transitioned from the sign of Aries to that of Pisces. (The astronomical transition to the constellation of Pisces, visible in the physical sky, had already occurred more than a millennium earlier. Here, we are talking about the sun's path through the more spiritual signs of the zodiac.)

According to Rudolf Steiner, this marked the beginning of the age of the consciousness soul, which can only be roughly indicated by such a date. First and foremost, we must describe that event as one that jolted humanity into an abrupt awakening in consciousness. Following Steiner's descriptions, let us attempt a brief characterisation.

When people in ancient and medieval times thought thoughts, they did so with the awareness that they were participating in a rich thought life that belonged not to themselves alone but to the angelic world. That is why the experience of thought in these older times was always associated with a feeling of reverent reception. When we say of a thought today that 'it dawns on us', or we find it 'enlightening', we are using an expression that would have been entirely appropriate for characterising the thought life of those ancient times. Thoughts shone into people's souls from outside.

Then the time came when the higher beings responsible for

administering the powers of thought in the cosmos, or the cosmic intelligence as it is known, allowed it to descend to human beings who by it were to find the path to freedom. From then on, people had to generate thoughts themselves. The 'I think' experience arose. As unfamiliar as such ideas may be, one must nevertheless dare to describe the process this way. The cosmic intelligence, which until then had been carried by the divine beings of higher worlds, rained down upon the earth.

Again, we might ask what feelings the Archangel Michael had looking upon that process. The gift that heaven now gave to humanity was a double-edged one. When people themselves became administrators of the powers of thought, freedom entered their being like a thunderstorm. But it was precisely because of this freedom that the great question arose. Will people take these freely given powers of thought and cultivate a cleverness that they will use to serve their egoism? Or will they awaken to the spirit and, out of sacrifice and in loving service to others, turn the powers of thought into organs for seeing God? The possibility of the most monstrous aberrations arose in a new and sudden way, as did the possibility of an unimagined higher development. A profound cosmic apprehension now took hold of Michael, who always strives for humanity's Christian future. Michael's suspense is replaced by Michael's concern.

To continue our reflection, we must refer to the alphabet of images in the Revelation to John. The language of the Apocalypse is so difficult for the earthly mind to grasp because we cannot imagine the pictures described as having been seen with human eyes. It is probably not wrong to say that the Apocalypse describes what the circle of archangels, and especially Michael, see with their eyes. We have this book in human language because John was allowed to see what the archangels see. This last book of the Bible contains the hands of the inner World Clock in its enormous cycles and rounds of epistles, seals, trumpets and bowls of wrath. We can read the laws of supersensible history from it. They are always valid but appear particularly clearly in specific manifestations at certain times. Thus, we can regard the age of the consciousness soul, into which humanity entered through that event at the beginning of the fifteenth century, in a special sense as the Age of Trumpets. What are the seven trumpet

3. BETWEEN TWO MICHAEL AGES

sounds from Michael's point of view? We can regard them as the great wake-up calls and warnings the archangel himself sends to alert humanity to the dangers that threaten it in the age of the consciousness soul. We hear Michael's tremendous concern when we listen to these sounds.

The Revelation to John introduces the sounding of the trumpets with a prelude. At the beginning of the eighth chapter we are shown a majestic and peaceful image in the open heavens:

> When he opened the seventh seal, there was silence in
> heaven for about half an hour. And I saw the seven angels
> who stand before God, and seven trumpets were given to
> them. Another angel, who had a golden censer, came and
> stood at the altar. He was given much incense to offer,
> with the prayers of all God's people, on the golden altar
> in front of the throne. The smoke of the incense, together
> with the prayers of God's people, went up before God
> from the angel's hand. (Rev. 8:1–4)

We are given an insight into the greatness and solemnity of the cultus performed in the heavens. We would like to think that nothing in the world can break through this devotion and silence, yet we already see the seven angels standing ready with the trumpets. We begin to anticipate that the moment is coming when the silence will be broken, namely when the angels raise their trumpets and make them sound. As it progresses, the Apocalypse itself brings movement into the tranquil picture:

> Then the angel took the censer, filled it with fire from
> the altar, and hurled it on the earth; and there came peals
> of thunder, rumblings, flashes of lightning and an earth-
> quake. Then the seven angels who had the seven trumpets
> prepared to sound them. (Rev. 8:5f)

A tremendous cosmic storm breaks out as the angel pours the fire from the heavenly altar and lets it rain down on the earth. The sounds of the trumpet are born from the thunder of that storm. These are the images through which the Apocalypse describes the event of the outpouring of the cosmic intelligence, which reached its decisive climax at the beginning of the fifteenth century.

Before we turn to the ages introduced by the sounding trumpets, let us look for a moment into the events that took place on earth while the outpouring of the rain of fire began in the spiritual worlds. Not much attention has been paid to the history of the fifteenth century, but that is probably due to the many tumultuous upheavals that were initially caused on earth by those supersensible events.

In a sense, the first half of the fifteenth century was characterised by the so-called Reform Councils that met in Pisa, Constance and Basel between 1409 and 1449, with brief interruptions. The leading personalities of Western Christianity, cardinals, bishops and professors, gathered to establish a new era of Christian life. One would think that this would have prepared humanity in the best possible way to receive the spiritual rain that poured down upon the earth. But if we look at the course of the council negotiations, we see only endless, hopeless arguments. Turning against the sole rule of the pope, which had already become quite contentious, nothing else emerged other than the idea, albeit modern, of a council. A form of ecclesiastical parliamentarism emerged. A hundred years later, Luther also invoked the councils against the pope, and that marked the beginning of the democratic impulse that played such a significant role in the further development of Europe. Its origins lie not on political but on ecclesiastical grounds. We are thus faced with the question: is this abstract modern idea the only thing that humanity could absorb from the fiery powers of thought in heaven?

The heavenly fire was also burning on earth around this time in the likes of Czech theologian Jan Hus and his friend and co-worker, Jerome of Prague. In 1415 the Church authorities decided that Communion wine should no longer be given to the laity. Jan Hus and Jerome of Prague, enthusiastic champions of inner freedom, continued to distribute the wine during the sacrament. For their defiance, they were both burned at the stake. The pyre the church authorities lit was an earthly fire that countered the rain of fire from heaven. That makes it clear how little humanity was prepared to receive what heaven had to give.

In 1431, the fire of a historic pyre flared up again. In Rouen

3. BETWEEN TWO MICHAEL AGES

in France, Joan of Arc, the Maid of Orleans, was burnt to death. The true spark of heavenly fire had ignited in the soul of that simple country girl. She had seen the Archangel Michael appear before her, and the words he spoke to her had inspired in her the superhuman enthusiasm and strength that enabled her to lead the French troops to victory. The dignitaries of this world had her burnt as a witch. Once again, the defensive fire of humanity, not open to heaven, blazed up.

In this context, there is one episode that has become less well known. There was a brilliantly talented young man in the French army known as Gilles de Rais. He had used his wealth to recruit troops with whom he fought in the French army against the English. His brilliant talent meant he was already Marshal of France by the age of twenty-five. The Maid of Orleans was placed under his personal protection while she led the army. After Joan of Arc's death, a striking change occurred in Gilles de Rais's character. Those who saw him during the day might have thought he had become a fanatical ascetic, for he devoted himself to the most ardent mortifications and penances. At night, however, in his castles in western France, the wildest orgies and debauchery took place. In Gilles de Rais, we have before us the first extreme version of a double life. The nocturnal-satanic side of his existence increased. He became a black magician, and before he met his end in 1440, he is said to have slaughtered around two thousand newborn children with his own hands in connection with the black magic rituals he practised.[1] Such infernal escalations of evil in the human world can only be understood if we look at what is happening simultaneously in the spiritual realm. If great things happen in the supersensible, a person is either strong enough to make themselves a vessel and servant for them, or they fail and fall prey to the other extreme. The infernal counter-fire works through them.

However, sparks of the pure heavenly fire did catch in a few places. First and foremost, reference should be made here to that the great Western cardinal, Nicolaus Cusanus, and an experience he had while travelling across the Mediterranean in 1438. He was on his way home from Byzantium, where he had gone on behalf of the Church Council of Basel to negotiate between the Eastern and Western churches. At the sight of the starry sky, the spiritual world opened up to him and he received the inspiration for his philosophical groundwork, *De docta ignorantia* (On Scholarly Ignorance). He wrote the book in the seclusion of his Moselle homeland and published it in 1440. In it, Cusanus touched on the incredible transformation that had begun within human minds.

Also on that same ship in 1438 was the eighty-three-year-old Greek scholar Gemistos Plethon, who had gone to Rome as a counter-envoy of the Eastern Church. He had led the last Greek school of philosophy in Mistra, near ancient Sparta, and in 1440 he founded the Platonic Academy in Florence, which became a rich source of humanism and Renaissance culture.

The new impulses were picked up in other ways, too. For example, in 1415, Prince Henry the Navigator, at the age of twenty-one, set out from Portugal and came to the West African islands, thus providing the impetus for the fifteenth century's voyages of exploration, such as those of Vasco da Gama and Christopher Columbus. It is also not unrelated to the supersensible events of the time that in the same year that Nicolaus Cusanus' book was published and the Florentine Academy was founded, Johannes Gutenberg invented the printing press. We can question whether that invention, which more than anything else ushered in the new world, was really a blessing to humanity or whether it initiated a significant devaluation and flattening of intellectual life. Humanity caught the fire that rained down from heaven in such forms and shapes as it liked, which led to many great things, but also to many distortions.

The sounding of the trumpets one after another in the Apocalypse triggers the stages of a disaster. The image of fire hurled from the heavenly altar down onto the earth is presented in various ways. At the first trumpet, a fiery rain mixed with hail falls onto the earth and wreaks havoc. The fiery element remains with the second trumpet and the action also maintains its direction from top to bottom: a burning mountain falls from the sky and disaster spreads across the earth. At the third trumpet, a burning star falls from heaven, bringing further calamity. At the fourth, the middle trumpet, the disaster spreads to the upper sphere as the sun, moon and stars are darkened. The direction has reversed: the depths answer the heights. At the fifth trumpet,

3. BETWEEN TWO MICHAEL AGES

a star that has fallen from the sky is given the keys to the abyss. Clouds of smoke rise from the abyss and out of them come vast swarms of locusts that destroy all living things. With the sixth trumpet, the direction from below to above stops. The forces of the abyss transform into ghosts of war: horse-like creatures race across the earth, crushing everything in their path, their bluish steel armour making them look like machines. Finally, at the seventh trumpet, the sequence of disasters is completed. Two beasts appear, one out of the sea and the other out of the earth, after the dragon-conquering archangel and his hosts have overcome the adversarial powers in heaven and thrust them down into the depths.

How can it be that the gifts of heaven, poured out of the vessels of solemn high worship, wreak such havoc on earth? Doesn't it say in the Letter of James that 'every good and perfect gift is from above' (James 1:17), meaning that everything that comes from above is good?

The basic example of what comes from above is the human being itself. We are all of celestial origin, not according to our body, but according to our soul-spiritual nature, and at our birth, we bring a celestial star and the fiery energies of the higher world with us to earth. The difficult question of human life is how much of the original heavenly nature can survive and prevail in the earthly world against the all-too-human, the all-too-earthly. In modern times, the belief has arisen that human beings are exclusively a product of heredity and the environment: that is, of forces acting from below. If the human being's heavenly origin can be so completely forgotten, might we not eventually arrive at a time when this heavenly origin is no longer perceptible in human beings, even to themselves?

An honest reckoning with the human soul's heavenly origin would change many things in today's culture, especially in education. Every child carries a treasure trove of heavenly souvenirs in the depths of their being, consisting of nothing but deeply dreaming images. These are the images of everything the soul could see while still in the supersensible spheres. Images of the life of the angelic realms and the holy activities that take place there, and of the archetypes of earthly existence and events all slumber deep beneath the threshold of conscious memory. As children grow, it is imperative that they encounter something in their education that is similar to that treasure trove of images, something of a pictorial nature, especially something permeated by the breath of genuine art and religion. Children's hunger for images stems precisely from these supersensible souvenirs. This hunger must be satisfied so that the heavenly can resonate within them. When children are presented with abstract, intellectual, utilitarian thoughts with only earthly content instead of genuine, artistic and religiously inspired nourishment, the heavenly treasure in their soul cannot help but wither and dry up. This withering away must continue throughout their lifetime if a person does not constantly maintain and nourish a connection with their heavenly origin through the genuine cultivation of art and religion.

But the problem we face is a double-edged one. What we bring from the spiritual world not only withers and dies if it is left unnourished and uncared for, it also turns into its opposite. This can happen by degrees and in stages. For example, many people suffer from an inner restlessness that even likes to disguise itself as something highly moral: a never-resting urge to be active and helpful. Here, we already have the rumbling of a heavenly inheritance, which has not been shown the path to calm, meditative, religious and artistic devotion. It is an intensification of that inner restlessness when a roving sensuality drives people to become excessively entangled in earthly feelings and desires. Such sensuality was not originally evil, however. Rather, it is the result of a degeneration into which the human soul's heavenly inheritance has fallen, and for that very reason it could almost always be transformed and healed by a strong artistic and religious feeling. After all, even the criminal instinct is nothing but a turning into the opposite of what should be and what remains of our heavenly origin.

We are faced here with a strict fundamental law of human existence: what comes from above *is* good, but whether it remains so on earth depends on how it is received and nurtured. If it is wrongly received and the appropriate care neglected, the heavenly fire can turn into the smouldering flames of hell and the abyss. That is the warning of the seven trumpets.

*

3. BETWEEN TWO MICHAEL AGES

From there, let us look at the development of the modern era up to our present day and into the future. After that initial period in the fifteenth century, European humanity went through an epoch in which it was gifted with completely new intellectual enthusiasms. With the joy of discovery, it looked around at the world, which seemed to emerge as though from behind a dim veil. But the fire of enthusiasm for the new life of thought and perception was already mingled with the ice of deadly hailstones. In this, the mystery of the first trumpet emerges. The fire raining down from heaven mixes with hail. In the earthly sense, it is inconceivable that fire and hail mix because fire melts hail. This spiritual image draws our attention to the danger that threatens enthusiasm if it is only directed towards earthly objects. It is then inevitable that the mind's cold, killing element, focussed on earthly benefits, will interfere. Every enthusiasm will one day fizzle out and lead to disappointment if it does not contain the possibility of approaching the spiritual world.

A second evolutionary phase in modern times brought the astonishing development of natural science. In the age of Galileo and Copernicus, the second trumpet sounded. Once again, the fire of new thinking was burning everywhere. But the more people explored and learnt about the realms of earthly nature, the more their view of heaven, the supersensible world, was blocked. The world became stony and opaque to the spiritual. It was as if a stone mountain had fallen from the sky, albeit one engulfed in heavenly fire. This was the same period in which Albrecht Dürer created his classic engraving, *Melancolia I.* The concern of the Archangel Michael, which turns almost to resignation, could not be depicted more directly than in this work of art. Something very similar to the mountain fallen to earth is seen in the figure of the archangel, his weary head supported by his hand, a brooding expression on his face. Next to him is a large rock carved with the straight lines and flat planes of a crystal – the stone of resistance. Dürer's image expresses the second trumpet.

If the world became stony in the age of natural science, humanity itself decreased in the subsequent age of the enlightened bourgeoisie. The third trumpet causes a burning star to fall from the sky. It bears the name Wormwood because it is bitter and works as bitterness in the world. A further stage in the development of the self occurred at this time, but forces were at work that, like everything bitter, contract and make us small. A well-fed, self-sufficient bourgeois egoism entered humanity, which made people believe that they were great, but which, in reality, made them shrink mentally and spiritually.

Then came the time when the transcendent, spiritual splendour of the sun, moon, and stars was extinguished for an increasingly clever humanity. The more that earthly cleverness took possession of the human soul, the more the ability to perceive the supersensible finally died out.

The effect of the celestial eclipse would have been all the more terrible if, through the unique influence of other spiritual events, the star of German idealism and romanticism had not simultaneously appeared in the sky for a short time.

The time was already dawning when the abysses of human nature reacted to the new powers of thought. The depths hissed and bubbled as if drops of water had fallen on red-hot iron. The world of abstract thoughts haunted humanity ever more eerily in the nineteenth century. Through their thinking, people engendered forces of decay and depletion that attacked their life forces, much like when swarms of locusts descend on a verdant landscape.

At present, we are experiencing the rise of the sixth trumpet. Of course, we must go through all of this, including the fifth trumpet's swarms of locusts turning into ghostly war horses. But despite fulfilling all the earthly duties the present moment demands of us, we must not cease to reflect on what we have done with the powers of thought poured out by heaven. After all, we are expending extraordinary amounts of intelligence in seeking means of mutual destruction.

The great turning point comes with the sixth trumpet. The images of disaster intermingle with glimpses of salvation. Suddenly, the golden angel appears, standing with one foot on the ocean and the other on land, his countenance shining like the sun, his head surrounded by a rainbow of colours. He holds the little book in his hand and gives it to us to eat. The seventh trumpet then reveals not only the dragon and the beast from the abyss but also the Archangel Michael who defeats the dragon. The upper temple then becomes visible, with the circle of the

3. BETWEEN TWO MICHAEL AGES

twenty-four elders who sing the hymn of praise, and the crowd of 144,000 who honour the divine Lamb on the mountaintop.

We see the angel with the 'Eternal Gospel' flying through the heavenly spheres. We behold the woman clothed with the sun giving birth to her child and Christ returning on the cloud with the sickle to bring in the world's harvest.

How can we understand the great turning point of the sixth trumpet? If the gifts of heaven are not to become instruments of hell for us, we must once again pluck up the courage to turn directly to the spiritual world. We must receive the book from the angel's hand and eat it. That is, we must seek a new connection to the supersensible with the most direct forces of our human nature and permeate our thinking with it. John's Revelation shows that we will receive tremendous help if we set this goal for ourselves.

Now, following the Mystery of Golgotha and the later outpouring of the cosmic intelligence, the Archangel Michael once again assumes leadership of our age, drawing closer to the earth to help people when they strive for the spiritualisation of their nature. This fact presents religious life with a completely new task. Until now, when one met people who were particularly clever or especially equipped with the power of reason, they were often cold, calculating natures who, in the majority of cases, showed little warmth of heart. If, on the other hand, one met people with a singular warmth of heart and devotion, people with a distinctive Christian empathy in the old style, one could again recognise in the majority of cases that they were those who were not particularly concerned with the development of their intellectual powers. On the contrary, they were only too happy to leave the tasks of thinking to others. It should have been more obvious long ago where that would lead. We should have seen that if that trend continued, the powers of the intellect, which have now been handed over to humanity to administer, would slip to one particular side. They would end up in the hands of cold natures and, finally, in the power of the demons who arise wherever cold and heartless cleverness builds its inventions. It is precisely that part of humanity that has associated itself with the ideals of Christian piety that has been guilty of a tremendous sin of omission by evading the task of stewarding the intellect's powers. Ultimately, theologians invented a theory they believed could justify that world-historical sin of omission. They distinguished between belief and knowledge, and yet this only encouraged a pious laziness of thought. They wanted to settle on the island of faith and leave knowledge uncultivated without realising that that made them complicit in the rise of the most sinister demons.

Traditional church Christianity has not yet taken seriously the second great transformative event that stands at the beginning of the new age. Above all, it has not yet recognised the transformation as establishing a new, religious task for humanity. But that is the task that a Michaelic Christianity must set itself. Precisely where a devoted will and a love of Christ are most strongly alive, work must be done regarding thought. A proper stewarding of the intellectual powers entrusted to us can then occur as a Christianisation of thinking. The cold mind must be redeemed. With fiery powers of the heart, thinking can be transformed into an organ of actual spiritual cognition, an eye for a new vision of God.

In the previous Michael age, the archangel gave the light of thought from above in abundance. Now, during his present regency, he wants to give the fire of thought from within. We must not wait for a miracle that will simply come upon us one day, like the outpouring of the Holy Spirit. The outpouring of the powers of intelligence on humanity has long since taken place. It would have been up to humanity to make a holy spirit out of it instead of a demonised intelligence. It is still up to us whether something of the Whitsun fire can be kindled from the intelligence that has been poured into humanity. If we want to be Christians in the Michaelic sense, we must feel jointly responsible for the Holy Spirit's heavenly fire. We should not say that, amid the stormy vicissitudes of the present day, it is pointless drawing attention to such tasks that seem removed from practical life. Only those who struggle for the Michaelic spirit in their own souls will find the forces with which they can master their present destiny and fulfil today's ever-increasing tasks and duties.

4

Christian Ideals in the Age of Michael
(1940)

Every year at Michaelmas, as we walk over the leaves drifting down from the trees, the language of autumn penetrates deep into our souls. It is also the language of the Archangel Michael, whose feast we celebrate on the threshold of autumn. The archangel walks through our time as we walk through the streets. He, too, walks over what remains as the remnants of a perishing world and ponders a whole new world in his thoughts. Year after year, with the fading of nature, in the splendidly shining death of its life, autumn calls out to us to find the way from nature to the spirit.

But what nature experiences in autumn, it has also been experiencing for a long time in human beings. We bring a continuous dying-off, a declining, ageing element into nature's life through our way of life and activities. In doing so, we deprive ourselves of her benefits. It is not at all surprising that nature provides so little for us today. We have intervened too deeply in the life of nature in recent centuries, both in our scientific worldview and in the practical applications of civilisation, which has culminated in the monstrous developments of modern technology. The materialistic scientific worldview, which sees only animated matter in everything, is an insult to nature. We cannot insult someone one moment and then expect love and help from them the next. How can we receive love and support from nature when we regard her so disdainfully and unlovingly through the eyes of materialism?

On the other hand, people seek out so-called untouched landscapes to refresh and recuperate. But do these landscapes not have the same soul as the destroyed areas where humans live? Where we exploit the raw materials for our so-called culture, and where we ultimately only use the most advanced achievements of technology to commit the most unheard-of acts of destruction? A mother will not easily be able to show love and help to someone who has murdered her son or daughter. How should nature still be capable of giving us strength since she is indeed that mother?

However, the development of the scientific-technological age was nevertheless necessary. It is deeply rooted in the necessities of human development that human beings deprive themselves of nature's benefits, that they do what autumn symbolically does every year when it withdraws nature's bounty. We have spread a great autumn around us and are thus confronted with the strict demand that autumn makes of us every year: to seek other, new sources for our lives.

Yes, if nature no longer helps people, where should they turn to find the meaning of their existence?

The world events in which we are immersed open up an entirely different sphere from that of nature. Today, the forces of destiny are making themselves felt more aggressively than ever before, and we cannot escape them. As paradoxical as it may seem at first, since we cannot expect any happiness or relief from it, only dramatic hardship and distress, it is just in this sphere of destiny that we can and must find the meaning of our existence. It is there that we encounter the true powers and driving forces of existence. Whoever senses that high invisible beings are now storming through the world and that mighty divine hands have intervened in humanity's circumstances already suspect that the being who guides the dramatic fate of our time is the Archangel Michael himself. With the name Michael, we are indeed addressing the initiator of the destinies that are unfolding around us. By feeling something of the archangel's fiery energy, we have our first contact with a whole world of supersensible beings. A gap opens in the curtain that separates us from the higher worlds. Now we must turn our gaze away from nature towards the spiritual world that lies behind that curtain. The Michaelic destiny of our days says to us, 'Learn to live with the spirit!'

We must think about this challenge in three ways. First, we will look at the spiritual orientation necessary for this, then we will consider attitudes of soul, and, finally, we will look at how we shape our lives accordingly.

How do we find the fundamental spiritual orientation of our time? Every age has its task. In Plato's time, the many geni-

4. CHRISTIAN IDEALS IN THE AGE OF MICHAEL

uses of Greek intellectual life cultivated philosophy to explore the world of ideas. In the early Christian era, Christian teachers focused on understanding Christ's nature and the world of the divine hierarchies with the concepts then available to them. In the time of Galileo and Copernicus, the task of the age was to investigate the laws and phenomena of external nature and to make them subservient to the human spirit.

But what is the task of our time?

Today, humanity is in a completely new phase of spiritual development. We face tasks that we cannot understand with existing concepts. We must have the courage to reach for entirely new concepts and unusual forms of expression to understand what is happening – and what *has* to happen – today. Even if this seems fantastic to many contemporaries, one of the concepts that can help us comprehend the cognitive tasks of the present is the idea that epochs of time are led by a succession of archangels. They are the regents of the ages, guiding time spirits who give each age its inner character. Since the end of the nineteenth century we have been caught in the turbulence between two epochs. Gabriel, the archangel of the moon, has given way to Michael, the archangel of the sun. Certainly, these are supersensible facts that mean nothing to those who do not want to know anything about a supersensible world. But it is part of the inner nature of the present that we must begin to understand the supersensible. This has the following causes.

The Gabriel age lasted for three and a half centuries, roughly from the Reformation onwards. The task of that age concerned the exploration of external nature. Gabriel was the inspirer of natural science, which, during the centuries prior to his regency, had risen in greatness. However, it was in accordance with the will of the spiritual world that a tragic one-sidedness found its way into humanity through the materialistic stamp of the scientific worldview. Gabriel inspired people in such a way that, for a time, they devoted themselves entirely to materialistic thoughts. In John Milton's *Paradise Lost*, Gabriel is the archangel who stands guard at the gates of paradise with a fiery sword, refusing entry to human beings. This is a truth that applies at all times: Gabriel is the archangel who knows why humanity must be expelled from supersensible realms and confined to purely sense-perceptible reality. In a Gabrielic age, the gates of the supersensible are shut to humanity. However, these are not the gates of paradise alone, but also the gates of hell. For a period of three and a half centuries, humanity was left undisturbed by either gods or demons in its quest to explore the natural laws governing the external earthly world, including the course of the stars.

Because the gates of the supersensible world were closed, people developed the materialistic worldview. But we must not forget that this one-sidedness was in harmony with the spirit of Gabriel. During the Gabriel age, humanity had to close its eyes to the spiritual world.

Why did it have to be that way? By focusing exclusively on material existence and the cultivation of the scientific worldview, people were able to strengthen their ego and become more independent. Today, however, matters are quite different from what they were in the second half of the nineteenth century when people said that the world consists only of matter. Today, the eyes of humanity are once again free to perceive the living spirit; the supersensible is penetrating human souls once again.

Those who pay attention can clearly feel that extrasensory powers are surging through people today, but they dare not yet take seriously what they sense. Instead, they habitually repeat the long since expired motto of the Gabriel age: the world consists only of matter and molecules.

But since the end of the nineteenth century, when the Archangel Michael succeeded the Archangel Gabriel, an abrupt turnaround has occurred in humanity's development, the most extreme that ever can occur. For if humanity's task in the age of Gabriel was to investigate the sense-perceptible world, then our task in the Michael age is to turn and face the supersensible world. The spiritual world must once again come into our field of vision. Michael is not the archangel who expels people from paradise; he is the one who calls them back. He invites them to walk through the now open gates. But if the gates of paradise are open, so, too, are the gates of hell. The characteristic feature of Michael's age is that all floodgates are open, whether we know it or not. Because we still cling to concepts and habits of thought that belong to the Gabriel era, we will not be able to understand

4. CHRISTIAN IDEALS IN THE AGE OF MICHAEL

what is happening today in this new age of Michael if we do not rise to the challenge of focussing on the supersensible world. The angelic worlds do not force themselves upon our consciousness; nevertheless, they present us with a changed world that the old concepts are unable to deal with.

The ideals that were valid a century ago in the age of natural science no longer apply today; the time of materialistic natural science has expired. The gods of that epoch have become the adversaries that Michael now confronts. Today, the dragon of materialism works where Gabriel once worked, and if Michael is taking up the fight against the dragon and looking to us for help, then a breakthrough to a new spiritual worldview must be found. The question arises, are there people who can cast off ignorance and courageously take up the task of our age by directing their gaze towards the supersensible?

In the newspapers today we can read that we are in a 'transitional period'. Even if what we read is just witty journalism, perhaps there is some truth in it. Let me take a book review as an example. The book is not about political or military matters, and the reviewer feels he has to apologise for the fact that such a book is being published today. He says:

> To limit the concept of topicality to military and political events would be to atrophy it unduly. What has come to a dramatic head in the last few months before the eyes of an astonished world is ultimately only the expression of a secular upheaval breaking through into visibility ... It would be foolhardy to anticipate the future, but what can clearly be seen is how much the present time is in a period of transition, a transition that affects religious, moral, spiritual and mental forces no less than political ones.

Not only is this true, but it is even more valid than today's journalism is inclined to recognise. A spiritual tidal wave has swept over humanity, this is what we must say about the basic spiritual orientation of our time. The fundamental Christian ideal of the Michael age is the courage to know. We can no longer cling to the view that seeks to separate faith and knowledge, that places an inner, divine world accessible only to faith apart from a science that deals only with the external world. This clouds humanity and is already part of the dragon's world. The boundaries of knowledge that natural science and theology have erected must be broken through.

Human beings must no longer be aware of and interested only in the external aspects of nature; they must realise that spiritual forces are at work there. We must become aware of the supersensible in all kingdoms of nature. But by bridging the chasms that separate us from mysteries of the inner world, we must also encounter the spiritual forces that are active in the soul. Future Christianity must strive for awareness of the spirit in the face of all the questions that nature and destiny throw at us.

What attitude of soul, what attitude of thinking, feeling and willing is now in keeping with the Michael age? We must consider the tremendous change of mood sweeping through humanity today like a natural phenomenon accompanying a transformation of consciousness. An aversion to, even a hatred of, intellectualism has developed among people, with many no longer wanting to hear anything that sounds like academic intellectualism. The entire body of thought of the past few centuries seems to be coming to an end.

Most of what has been taught in schools and universities not only seems superfluous to some people now, but even ridiculous. Children no longer want to learn about ancient Greek or Roman history, for they are obsessed with technology. The elemental spirits of technology are at work in them and they are only interested in aeroplanes and cars. There is undoubtedly a lot to be said for the fact that some mummified educational methods are being abolished today. However, one must recognise and judge the process as a whole.

There are two kinds of thinking which, in antiquity, were portrayed in the myth of the brothers Epimetheus and Prometheus. Epimetheus was the weaker of the two and his name means 'afterthought' or 'hindsight'. He was always lagging behind in his thinking and understood only what belonged to the past and was no longer living. If a person thinks merely with their head, they are like Epimetheus. Such is 'head' reasoning; it lags behind the present life.

4. CHRISTIAN IDEALS IN THE AGE OF MICHAEL

The other kind of thinking comes more from the depths of the will and was personified by Prometheus, whose name means 'foresight' and who dared to steal fire from the gods to give to humanity. Today, when we turn away from intellectual thinking and focus one-sidedly on so-called practical thinking, we are reaching, albeit tentatively, for the region of Prometheus. His is the thinking that looks ahead. The thinking used in mathematics, physics and technology is constructive. It invents, and what it invents is impressive because its creations seem to be something new and future oriented. In that respect, it is understandable that today we have consigned the Epimethean thinking of grammar school and university to the dustbin of the past. As a child of the technological age, one wishes to be a comrade of Prometheus: the practical, inventive, technical genius who handles fire.

It is justified to feel that way today. A Promethean element must be gained. Epimetheus and Prometheus behave, in some respects, like Gabriel and Michael. Properly understood, the Promethean element is related to Michael. In the Michael age, we must develop a thinking imbued with the power of the will that serves life by intervening creatively in the world. But humanity does not know what it is doing when it develops the kind of one-sided will-thinking that has produced our modern technology. It does not acknowledge the sinister spaces into which it is venturing. It does not know that it is playing with the Promethean fire, the use of which requires more than external, technical expertise.

First of all, it is a fact that modern technology, despite its admirable greatness, has also surrounded us with much that is of a sinister nature. Through it, we increasingly find ourselves in the position of the sorcerer's apprentice, who cries out in despair: 'I can't get rid of the spirits I have summoned.' Even during the initial offensives during the Second World War, as the most modern technological achievements were put to use, one could read in the newspapers that a veritable hell had been unleashed. The word 'hell' was already part of the everyday vocabulary used to characterise our work of destruction and annihilation.

As the war progressed, the horror that humanity had brought upon itself increased. The systematic destruction of cities continued, and even though it was thought the limits of what was possible had been exceeded, a terrifying new scale of destruction was achieved at the very end when the first atomic bombs fell. Finally, there was no avoiding the realisation that the hasty perfection of technology had torn open spheres of the abyss whose sinister mysteries were breaking into human existence.

To shed some light on these fathomless questions, I would like to approach them from an angle that might at first glance seem overly lyrical. Today, we need new insights into how the three powers of the soul – thinking, feeling and willing – relate to each other in human beings. Conventional psychology has only inadequate concepts for this. With its learned abstractions, it is of no use to us. We need to take a much more realistic, inner view.

Thinking, feeling and willing are the three fundamental forces in our souls. But how different they each are! Only in thinking are we awake. In feeling and willing, on the other hand, we carry around with us the mysteries of the night, even when we are busy with our daily work. Rudolf Steiner often spoke about this. In our waking consciousness it is day, in our feeling life we dream, and in our willing we are asleep, there it is night. This is why people today talk about the 'subconscious' and 'unconscious' in human beings.

Now, a strange longing has come to light in modern humanity over the last century. It is the longing to penetrate from the glaring light of day of ordinary head-consciousness into the deeper, more nocturnal regions of the soul. Let us look at three testimonies of this longing for the night. Friedrich Nietzsche puts these words into the mouth of his Zarathustra:

> O man, notice!
> What does deep midnight say?
> I slept, I slept –
> I am awakened from deep dream:
> The world is deep
> And deeper than the day had thought.[1]

What our waking mind can think exists only on the surface of reality. The world's true mysteries lie deeper than our daytime minds, and can only be unravelled by our soul's deeper, nocturnal powers.

4. CHRISTIAN IDEALS IN THE AGE OF MICHAEL

The poet Novalis has already given perfect expression to the same longing in his *Hymns to the Night*: 'Aside I turn to the holy, unspeakable, mysterious Night.'

This turning away must be complete. We must even turn from the marvellous lights of the night sky because they are still reminders of the lights of the day:

> More heavenly than those glittering stars we hold the
> eternal eyes which the Night hath opened within us.
> Farther they see than the palest of those countless hosts
> – needing no aid from the light, they penetrate the depths
> of a loving soul – that fills a loftier region with bliss
> ineffable ... He who has stood on the mountain frontier
> of the world, and looked across into the new land, into
> the abode of the Night – truly he turns not again into the
> tumult of the world, into the land where dwells the Light
> in ceaseless unrest.[2]

We not only have our physical eyes, we also have eyes that 'the night has opened in us'. These eyes are initially closed, but when they are opened they allow us to look into the sphere to which we belong with our feelings and will. With them, we perceive a larger, more important world.

Richard Wagner serves as the third witness of this metaphysical nocturnal longing. In *Tristan and Isolde*, he starts with the high song of the night's secrets. In Act Two, Tristan sings of the love potion's magic:

> He opened up to me,
> The blissful realm of the night
> In which I otherwise only woke dreaming.
> From the image in the heart's mountainous shrine
> he scares away the day's deceptive glow,
> That night-sighted, my eye may see it true.

Our spiritual eye must become 'night-sighted' if we are to see the truth. The longing for the realm of the soul's deeper powers cannot express itself more clearly. In reality, what appears to be a personal longing for love has become transparent for the human soul's most comprehensive, supra-personal striving for life, as Tristan sings:

> Oh, now we were
> night consecrated!
> The treacherous day,
> the envy-ready day,
> His deception could separate us,
> But his lies no longer deceive!
> His vain splendour,
> His boastful glamour
> scorns, to whom the night
> consecrates his gaze.

Such passages express the sacred magic that works when human beings descend into the well of feeling and willing where the light of daytime thought dims. It is there that they come close to the angelic world.

In addition, a completely different stream has come to the fore, one that has taken hold of our materialistic thinking with all the instinctive nature of the will. As has already been mentioned, this has given rise to a contempt for the intellectual and a deep abhorrence of intellectualism, which itself has led to a passionate turning towards what is instinctive and unconscious.

At the same time, the opinion has emerged that the more closely one investigates the physical human being, the more clearly it appears that we are related to the animal. The animal is believed to sit in the depths of human nature as its actual ancestor. By idolising what is unconscious and instinctive, which is often misleadingly called the 'intuitive', we allow what is animal in us to assume primacy over what is human. For if instincts determine the value of human beings, what then are human beings? Because animals far surpass us in instinctive power, it is believed by some that our head-thinking has weakened our instinctual nature and thereby disrupted our essential being. According to this view, human beings are animals that have fallen into decadence. So, who is right? The poetic geniuses, with their enthusiasm for the spiritual secrets of the night who recognise that human beings reach into the angelic world with the more profound powers of

4. CHRISTIAN IDEALS IN THE AGE OF MICHAEL

their souls? Or those who worship instinct and who believe they are praising human beings when they say that our deeper nature is related to animals?

Dogmas must not be erected today, yet certain dogmas must be overthrown. And the dogma that must be overthrown first and foremost is that humanity descended from animals. We are not descended from animals! Only extreme materialism could elevate that to a dogma.

Human beings are of a spiritual nature: our true essence originates in higher worlds. Recognising this is one of the most urgent tasks of our time. Our divine origin is why the deeper forces of our soul, our feeling and willing, dive down into the ocean of angelic powers within us. With our heads, we protrude freely out of the water. With our feelings and willing, we are immersed in the ocean of divinity. That is why poets have always felt the night to be sacred.

This brings us to a difficult truth. With our deeper soul forces we reach into the supersensible world. But today when we reach into the supersensible world it can all too easily happen that anti-divine forces, what mythology calls the 'beast from the abyss', take hold of us. This occurs when we reach into the sphere of the will in a materialistic way, which we do through technology.

We have trained our thinking to be more practical and imbued our thoughts with the power of the will. But we have placed these thoughts in the service of our outer earthly life with all its expediencies and egoisms. Meanwhile, the supersensible world, which remained close to humanity in earlier times, has withdrawn. But one cannot penetrate the sphere of the will and remain solely in the earthly material realm. Humanity believed it was creating purely earthly futures by using the thoughts of the will to make inventions. In reality, however, we have reached into the sphere of the supersensible and conjured up the 'beast from the abyss'. This is why we must so urgently fight the theory of our descent from animals. It not only opens the door to beastliness in humans, but also to the beastly demons of the deep.

The dragon against which Michael fights pervades contemporary human culture. Overthrowing the dragon is the task of the Michael age.

People today have swung from one extreme to the other. It is right that intellectualism should be overcome; we must turn away from the Luciferic illusions of the purely intellectual mind. But now humanity has succumbed to the other extreme, which is all the more dangerous because it brings us into the realm of the Ahrimanic-satanic powers that reside in technology. In the machines of the technological age, we encounter the 'beast from the abyss'.

At first glance, the slogans about overcoming intellectualism have something captivating about them. In the era of extreme cerebral brilliance, the sphere of feeling was pushed aside as being overly sentimental; our dream life was also neglected in the name of cleverness. The counterattack of the will, however, subjects everything to the control of technology. We are threatened with nothing remaining of our dream life except chaotic nightmares. We have disturbed the miraculous realm of the night by stirring up the powers of night within our own nature. Instead of gracious forces that build us up and refresh us in our sleep, we are approached at night by the ghosts we ourselves have conjured.

There will be no salvation if we replace Epimethean head-thinking with the Promethean-technical thinking that rushes ahead. We must establish a balance between the powers of the human soul by building a bridge between thinking and willing. We must not lose faith in thinking. The warmth of the blood must enter the cool thoughts of the head, and vice versa: we must illuminate the thoughts of the will with the clear light of ideals instead of merely following the expediency of external existence. We must not reach into the sphere of will without reverence. We must want and know that we meet the angels when we allow ourselves to be given thoughts from the sphere of the will.

In the Michael age, we face the task of slowly awakening the deeper soul forces within us. It is of the greatest importance that we consciously undertake to educate our feelings, which form the centre of our being between thinking and willing. This middle sphere is almost entirely absent in modern human beings. There are those who, out of an aversion towards sentimentality, deliberately cultivate a lack of feeling. As a result, the feelings

4. CHRISTIAN IDEALS IN THE AGE OF MICHAEL

they think they do have are all too often either disguised intellectualisms or the drives and passions that belong to the will. We must cultivate the feeling centre of our being so as not to be torn apart between the extremes of the head and mere wilfulness. Here, we encounter the tasks of the artistic and religious life, which we cannot take seriously enough. This must bring about a progressive awakening in us. A gentle sunrise of awakening consciousness must first illuminate the sphere of feeling in which we only dream. Then, with awareness and wakefulness, we must gradually penetrate the sphere of the will, wherein we are still asleep.

Richard Wagner followed up *Tristan and Isolde* with *The Mastersingers of Nuremburg*, adding to the high song of the night the radiant song of a new daytime enthusiasm. Everything in *The Mastersingers* is so sunny, and the sun's brightness is finally crowned in the radiant chorus, 'Wake up! The day is nigh.' Richard Wagner has secretly poured his entire philosophy into this work.

In the drama, the knight Walter von Stolzing has a dream on St John's night. In the morning, he relates it to Hans Sachs, the old master singer, who instructs the knight to translate the dream into poetry and music. In doing so, he expresses Richard Wagner's deepest conviction:

> My friend, this is the poet's work,
> That he should remember and read his dreams.
> Believe me, man's truest madness
> Is revealed to him in a dream,
> All creative writing and poetry
> Are nothing but true dream interpretation.

The one who sang about the night and its secrets in *Tristan and Isolde* now teaches us about the mystery that reigns on the threshold between night and day, between sleeping and waking. True art is born when human beings awaken from a dream, or rather *in* a dream. The dream sphere is the womb of art. But to attain its blessings, we must quietly awaken where we otherwise merely dream, only then can the inspirations of heaven penetrate earthly life.

But our gentle awakening in the dream sphere must also give birth to a piety towards the future. The religions of past ages were rooted and remained in the unconscious layers of human nature. The piety of the ages that lie behind us rightly belonged to the night-time realm, governed by the angels under the guidance of a higher spiritual power. That spiritual power, which we can think of as the regent of the night, is known in the Bible as Yahweh, whose symbol was the moon. The regent of the night was the regent of religious life. In the past, the saying 'The Lord gives to his own in their sleep' (Psalm 127) was a revealing truth.

But that is precisely one of the reasons why modern people no longer want anything to do with religion. Modern humans do not want to sleep; they want to wake up. The fact that they reject all sleep-related devoutness can also be seen in the poisonous, hate-filled slogan that religion is the opiate of the people. A religion that reduces the degree of wakefulness can no longer benefit us. Religious life must pass from the dominion of Yahweh to another dominion. The archangel of Yahweh is Gabriel, who is the archangel of the moon. We must liberate religious life from the dominion of Yahweh and Gabriel and pass into the sphere of Michael, the archangel of the sun, who is the patron of true awakening.

Through Michael, the divine entity who replaced Yahweh becomes the guide of the new religious life. This is Christ himself. Christ is the sun spirit, and Michael, the archangel of the sun, stands in his direct service. We must find the transition from the moon to the sun in religious life if the step from Yahweh to Christ is to happen. In the last two thousand years, although the name of Christ was already on everyone's lips, we still had a Yahweh-style piety. Religious life was not yet dominated by Christ, the sun spirit. It was still under the sign of the moon, and the subconscious gave religious life its colour and character.

Why is it that theologians of all churches have always been so upset when people have spoken of Christ as the sun spirit? It is because they do not want to emerge from the church's unacknowledged slumber. They are not prepared to reorganise religious life, which is still thoroughly dominated by the old laws of the unconscious.

*

4. CHRISTIAN IDEALS IN THE AGE OF MICHAEL

In the Michael age, we must cultivate an entirely new religious mood. We need a religious life that goes hand in hand with an alert thinking that can guide our feelings into the bright sunlight of our awareness. The awakening of feeling through the cultivation of a new religious life will also enable us to awaken in the sphere of the will, which will restore harmony to humanity. For those of us who have fallen blindly into this stormy age, the only salvation is the deliberate creation of a conscious religious life. This is especially true today since all religious legacies have been exhausted.

The legend of 'The Key', found in Albrecht Schaeffer's book *The Secrets*, describes how a new religious life helps a person take hold of the darker side of human cognitive powers in the proper way. It tells of a traveller who, on his life's journey, seeks the city of God on earth, which he heard about as a child. One day, as the sun is setting after a long and arduous journey, he sees the domes and towers of the city of God on the horizon. Reinvigorated, he strides forwards. Night falls around him, but he continues to see a single shimmering light in the distance. Eventually, he comes to a gate set in the large, high wall that encircles the city. Through the keyhole shines the light he saw from a distance. The traveller knocks. A small window opens in the gate and that bright light pours out. In the golden haze, he sees many thousands of luminous figures.

An angel stands in front of the window, holding out a loaf of bread, and says, 'Take and eat!' But the traveller replies, 'I do not desire food; I desire entrance.' The angel closes the window, leaving the traveller outside in the dark.

The traveller continues on his way. He follows the wall as it curves slowly round, hoping that he will come to another gate through which he can gain entry. But the wall stretches on, and soon the traveller becomes tired. After a long time, he finds himself back at the same gate. Again, the traveller knocks, and again the angel appears at the window and hands him the loaf of bread.

'Take and eat!' the angel says.

'I do not desire food; I desire only admission,' the traveller responds once more, and once more the angel closes the window.

Angry and exhausted, the traveller sets off again.

Arriving at the gate for the third time, he knocks. The angel hands him the bread.

'Take and eat!'

Now the traveller is so tired that he takes the bread. He sinks down against the wall, so tired that he is already falling asleep and drifting off into a dream, and says, 'What more could anyone want but a loaf of bread from God's city and to sleep at the foot of its wall!' The traveller is hungry, and before he falls asleep he breaks the bread, and behold, out falls the key with which he can now unlock the gate himself.

This legend provides us with an essential insight into the nature of the new religious life we need to achieve. The first step we must take in seeking God is to learn to be receptive to divine grace and allow ourselves to be fed from the spiritual world. These days, as self-confident, ego-endowed human beings, we can all too easily fall into the trap of believing that we can sustain ourselves in everything we do, that we do not require help of any kind. In the image of the bread offered to the traveller by the angel, the legend hints at the sacramental character that the contemporary devotional life must have. Through careful striving and participation in sacramental life, we awaken in our feelings the power that then helps us to awaken in the depths of our will.

Through the organs of awakened feeling and will, human beings come face to face with the beings of the spiritual world. We participate in the sphere of the cosmic-divine will, not in an external Promethean sense, but in an inner Michaelic one. The key is in our hands; we can unlock the gate to the spiritual world if we want.

Technology, with its focus on earthly achievements, comes into being through the impetuous, Promethean grasp of the willed thoughts of untransformed human beings. Technology believes it can bring the future into the present with its discoveries and inventions, though in reality it creates nothing but an intensified impermanence, as each state-of-the-art invention is superseded by the next in a headlong rush of development. If, on the other hand, Christian apocalyptic thinking and perception awaken in the soul, a new vision of the future will open up before us. Prophetic abilities will become active that are already heralded by the fact that human beings, while remaining in the

4. CHRISTIAN IDEALS IN THE AGE OF MICHAEL

realm of thought, nevertheless learn to read nature and the signs of the times in a fundamentally new way. The spiritual that governs nature and destiny will open up before us.

Apocalyptic thinking is the antithesis of technical thinking, although once we achieve it, we will be able to affirm technology completely. For then we will be able to place technology in the service of humanity's true spiritual goals. We will be able to read the apocalyptic sign language of the technology we have created. People don't realise it, but with our technology we are creating Ahrimanic counterimages of what exists in the supersensible world. It is true that we can no longer do without technology, but we must use the powers at work in it to further the progressive goals of the world. Otherwise, we risk losing ourselves to those powers.

The Christian Community's task is to cultivate a religious life that enables people to cope with technology and its spectres. The devotional life we strive for must be guided by the motto, 'Wake up! The day is drawing near!' In the most genuine spiritual sense, an awakening Christianity must come to life among us. With the awakening of the soul's deeper, nocturnal powers, Michael, the archangel of the sun, becomes active in our hearts. Such an awakening will be fulfilled when the whole of humanity is glowing with the fire of the spirit that shines out of the human heart: Christ himself, whose archangel is Michael. Only then does it become true that Christianity is the true religion of the sun, in the sense of an inner light kindled with spiritual courage.

Finally, let us turn to the issue of life in the Michael age. Today, the ideal of self-creative activity has taken hold of the greater part of humanity. People no longer want to live passively; they want to play an active part in the creation of their own lives. Two obstacles stand in the way of this ideal, however. The first is the fundamental error that places us close to animals as a mere product of heredity. Animals' instincts surpass that of human beings to such an extent that humans appear weak and decadent in comparison. As long as we idolise blood-born instincts, we work to bury the source of true activity in human beings. This lies in the spiritual being of our I, which utilises the blood only as a tool and is precisely what distinguishes us from animals.

The second obstacle is traditional religious life, which is fundamentally passive in nature. One might argue that much has been accomplished by people who live religious lives. They have built hospitals and provided significant social aid, for example. But that activity has always been carried out on the margins, so to speak; it was not developed within the field of religion itself. There, pious feelings have been rendered largely passive by a theology that speaks of the exclusivity of grace through which human beings receive everything from God and to which they can add nothing. We must understand this religious mood rightly. It was the Archangel Gabriel who had an interest in passive human religiosity. In the age of Gabriel, it was right to experience religious feeling exclusively as a gift from God that was bestowed on us by nature. At that time, it was said that this or that person had a religious nature, and those who did not could do nothing about it. This was justified in the age of Gabriel because a piety stemming from an inherited nature was needed to balance out the materialistic effects of what was being cultivated as natural science. But as long as this continued to be the case, it was inevitable that religion and science would eventually diverge.

In the Michael age, it must be different. The religious heritage of the old days is over. Of course, some people still have an inherited treasure of religious power, and such inheritances must not be squandered. But today, people generally depend on starting anew, on recreating a sphere of religious feeling within themselves. In the Michael age, religion, in its innermost essence, must be sustained by soul activity. We are no longer religious by nature; instead, we must follow a particular inner path to become devout again. This deliberately cultivated religious life does not contradict grace, rather it shows how truly profound the mysteries of grace are. If we can kindle a spark in our soul, then religious life will illuminate the cloudy meaning of our existence. We will begin to open the eyes of our souls. Where before we saw only plants in the meadows or blossoms on the trees, we will discover the creative deeds of spiritual beings.

It is an important stage of living with the spirit that we not only begin to love the divine in nature again, but that we also learn

4. CHRISTIAN IDEALS IN THE AGE OF MICHAEL

to *see* it. In Christianity, all talk of bread and wine, which have such a central meaning, must sound radically different depending on whether the speaker has only a human conception of Jesus or whether they understand that Christ is a cosmic being. If it was only the human Jesus who celebrated the Last Supper with his disciples, then the bread and wine remain external elements and we cannot understand the mystery of transubstantiation. But if we begin to understand that Christ is a cosmic being, then we can find him within bread and wine: the spiritual and the natural permeate each other and do not remain separate. Unless the light of a new religious life shines into nature, Christianity cannot persist. A cosmic Christianity must come to life among us. The religious life of the past, alienated from nature, can no longer give us what we need today. By way of the new religious life, we find the nature that we previously lost, and to the devout, all of nature will then be bread and wine.

Our inner eye must also open to the secrets of destiny. In the age of Gabriel, humans only saw destiny as God's reward or punishment. Happiness was a reward, misfortune a punishment. In the Michael age, we must learn to recognise the hand of God's love even and especially in misfortune. We will then understand the relentless severity of Michael, who lets us get caught up in catastrophes and suffering precisely when we are supposed to be brought inwardly closer to God. A heroic Christianity will emanate from such a perception and recognition of destiny's powers and intentions. A Christianity that does not find a connection to the power of Michael will lose all spiritual significance; it may even disappear.

However, taking the spiritual element of destiny into account leads to what is most important in shaping life: human beings learning to live again with the spiritual aspect of their own human essence. All the battles currently being fought are ultimately about human beings, and they are fought for human beings. Michael is the patron of humanity who preserves the human ideal in the supersensible world. But what do we know about ourselves today?

We must learn to know ourselves as supersensible beings related to the divine. The dragon, of course, is also in us, which is why we must take Michael increasingly into our hearts. We must expect the divine to enter the human sphere in a very concrete way. The belief in the human being as the offspring of the divine is one of the prerequisites for a concrete life in the spirit. New sources of love will open up to us when we learn to recognise in every person we meet, whether we like them or not, a supersensible, God-related being. Every human being, no matter how they may outwardly appear, is in their true essence of a supersensible nature.

As this new power of love emerges between human beings as we recognise the divine in each other, it will have an impact on the social sphere where, as in traditional religion, the old powers are exhausted. The 'Christ in us' will be the unifying factor from person to person. The Archangel Michael, who today is a time spirit and no longer the folk spirit of a single people, as in earlier times, is concerned with the whole of humanity. We, too, must therefore cultivate an interest in humanity as an essential ideal of the Michael age.

Destiny compels us to interact with the supersensible world because the 'gods' closest to us are our own deceased loved ones. In the early days of the war, I received a strikingly large number of letters from women who had lost someone close to them. Repeatedly in their letters they stated that, following the loss of a loved one, they felt the same as when they were expecting a child. They described a similarity between the state of pregnancy and the state one enters into with the death of someone close.

This touches on a deep mystery. When a person has died, we no longer see them. When a mother carries a child under her heart, she does not see them either. The soul of a deceased person can be in us just as the soul of the unborn child is in the mother. The person who has just died wants to be a seed. They want something to be born from their death. Deeds are to be done that we could not do alone if we did not have our deceased helpers in the spiritual world.

Life with the deceased opens the gates to a rich life with the divine world in general, something we must achieve in the Michael age. Just as we learn to live with the deceased by feeling them within us, so must we also learn to feel the higher beings of the spiritual world within us, too, including Michael and Christ himself. The words 'Christ in you' and 'Christ in us' in the liturgy

4. CHRISTIAN IDEALS IN THE AGE OF MICHAEL

of The Christian Community are not mere wishes but light-filled fulfilments.

When we learn to live with the spirit in this way – in nature, in destiny, in ourselves and other human beings, with the deceased and the other beings of the spiritual worlds – a Michaelic quality enters our lives. When we then say, 'Christ in us,' we can also say at the same time, 'We in Christ.' We feel Christ in our own inner being and can sense that Christ has come very close to humanity. More veils will fall away, revealing the richness of the supersensible world that is already permeating human life today. Eventually, the veils will part fully, and Christ will appear in his clear spiritual form.

In the previous pre-Christian Michael age, the archangel placed messianic prophecies and premonitions in the souls of those prophetic human spirits. In today's Michael age, he leads us to the second Christ event, the return of Christ. As we learn to recognise Michael in the storm of present-day destinies, Michael himself becomes a rent in the veil for us. We recognise him: he is the countenance of Christ. Only a thin veil needs to become transparent where he stands, and Christ will appear before us. The time has come when this can and must become our experience. Humanity can and must become clairvoyant again for the sphere of the spirit. Then we will see that being who brings comfort and healing, and who alone can help us cope with the difficult tasks facing us in these stormy times.

5

The Michael Age in Autumn
(1945)

In all of world history, there has probably never been an age whose destiny has been as difficult to understand as the one in which we are now living. Countless lives have come to a violent end, and entire streams of historical development that had stood secure for millennia have been destroyed. If we only look at the earthly realities, we really cannot understand the meaning of our time. We are faced with irresolvable riddles.

But if we raise our eyes to a higher plane, perhaps a glimmer of light can fall from those beings who direct our earthly destiny from out of the invisible. Perhaps then we can hope to understand something of God's intentions for us and our time.

From the spiritual world, beings from the rank of the archangels take it in turn to guide human history. In cooperation with higher powers, each archangel leaves his mark on the age. Towards the end of the nineteenth century, a radical change occurred in humanity. Gabriel, the archangel of the moon, had been guiding humanity for some three and a half centuries at that point. Then, in 1879, he was succeeded by the Archangel Michael, the archangel of the sun.

What does it mean that we have moved from the age of Gabriel to the age of Michael? These names no longer mean anything to modern humans, who have lost all knowledge of supersensible beings. We must learn to think and envision anew the beings whose names these are. People used to know that Gabriel was the stern archangel who had once driven people out of paradise. Michael is also strict, but his task is to return people to paradise, as the angel's words in the old Christmas play suggest: 'I will recall you late and slow.' But we might ask, how can it be that in our time the spiritual power that leads people back to paradise is at the helm? Are we not being driven further from paradise with each day?

5. THE MICHAEL AGE IN AUTUMN

Even if we have not fully realised it yet, humanity has long since been expelled from the paradise of nature and true art. Today, we are also being relentlessly driven out of the paradise of bourgeois cosiness and comfort. The world is becoming increasingly *un*-paradisal. The expulsion from paradise seems to have only just been completed in our time.

And yet, if we focus on the spiritual, everything is reversed. When Gabriel reigns, he has the task of leading people into the earthly world. During his most recent rulership, humanity had settled into the earthly world. We built paradises on earth as best we could and felt so secure and comfortable in them that we forgot the true paradise from which we came. After all, though we humans are in this world, we are not of it; our true essence has entered this world as a foreigner from another sphere. It will require long and arduous labour to bring the lustre of the spirit into our life on earth so that this world may also become a home for us in our true nature. When people planted the all-too-earthly paradises of this world around them, then was the expulsion from paradise complete. We lost our connection with our sphere of origin; we finally forgot who we are. Now, when Michael declares these earthly paradises null and void and tears them apart, that is not an expulsion from a real paradise. He does so to make us remember the lost paradise of the spiritual world, or at least to make us yearn for it again as the world from which we came. Only in this way can we find ourselves again after losing ourselves to earthly things. The destruction around us – and this is the intention of the Michaelic zeitgeist – is to serve our repatriation into the world of the spirit. It is the world to which we belong according to our true nature, and which we must also manifest on earth.

Science and technology were developed during the age of Gabriel that now lies behind us. They are the gifts of the Archangel Gabriel to humanity. He taught people to find their way into the world of earthly things in a creative way, but that time has ended. It was not so long ago, only say until 1910 or 1914, that humanity could say, 'Look how far we have come!' After that time, however, people began to look more deeply into things and realised the shaky foundations on which that cultural pride stood. Today, it has been thoroughly refuted and exposed as a grandiose illusion – indeed, as a seduction by the ruler of this world.

From now on, people will no longer understand nature without focusing on the spiritual. Natural science, marvellously developed, will become shaky and uncertain. People will doubt the laws of nature because they will come across all kinds of phenomena in the universe that natural science can no longer explain. Nature itself will become an ever-greater enigma because people will not understand it if they do not consider the workings of the spiritual forces within it. Nor will people in the future be able to comprehend destiny if they remain mired in their materialistic thinking.

Today, our thinking has become bankrupt. People are tired of thinking, and many of the younger generations have given up thinking altogether. By thinking, I mean a vigorous, energetic thinking that seeks to take hold of the world and the spirit in it. But a person can only live superficially if they do not rekindle in the soul the courage to think. Just as it was the task of the Gabriel age to pursue natural science, it will be the task of the Michael age to develop spiritual science and add knowledge of the spirit to knowledge of nature. Everyone must struggle with a fervent heart to understand the spiritual connections of the world. Each one must feel that the world is held together only in its innermost depths where the experiments of natural science do not penetrate.

In our age, all endeavours to shape life and the world have reached a dead end. We have only learnt to organise life in terms of technology, but we are beginning to realise that this is also driving the last remnants of soul life out of human relationships.

What is the result of highly developed technology today?

Humanity now has the ability to destroy the world. In fact, it can no longer do anything else. It does not possess the means to bring about real reconstruction, even if it believes it does. Some hardships can be alleviated – and where we are able to do so, we must – but it is impossible to build up something living from merely earthly forces. One of the most astute thinkers at the end of the nineteenth century, Eduard von Hartmann, said that the consequence of the contemporary worldview was simply to dig a deep hole in the earth and fill it with the explosives that humanity was about to invent, and in that way blow up the entire globe.

5. THE MICHAEL AGE IN AUTUMN

That sounded fantastic at the time. But it was nothing more than a prophecy of the ability humanity has indeed acquired today. Fantasy has moved into the realm of technical possibility. Developing technology was in keeping with the tasks of the Gabriel age. Carrying it forward into the age of Michael as if nothing has changed for humanity, however, could well have disastrous consequences.

When the warm days begin to wane and autumn and winter approach, people take notice. They do not continue to wear their summer clothes, they dress more warmly. But when there is a change in the regency of the archangels, such as that which characterises our present time, people do not notice and carry on as if nothing had happened.

I feel compelled to describe a legend in which a person of the present could recognise themselves. It tells of a man, a brilliantly gifted inventor, who had a laboratory in his house. With his experiments, he was on the trail of a preparation with which he could produce as much artificial food as he wanted. He could also use it to create remedies that would cure all diseases. The man worked hard and produced a large quantity of this magic remedy. Unfortunately, the preparation was highly flammable and a spark from the fire in his hearth caused it to combust. It goes without saying that the man's joy over his amazing remedy was short-lived as the fire consumed not only his preparation but his house too.

This is where humanity finds itself today insofar as it still places its hopes in technology. In the Michael age, technology has become a double-edged sword. It becomes dangerous by becoming magical. The atomic bomb – its name is just the glorification of an unproven hypothesis – is the magical after-fruit of Gabriel in the age of Michael. Modern science's 'mole work' has uncovered a subterranean layer. We have accessed previously unknown forces that had remained under cosmic lock and key. It is the third force beyond magnetism and electricity, the force of disintegrating matter, exploding matter. Forces have been uncovered that are not of this world but are also not of a higher world; rather, they are of a subsensible nature.

Just as we must add the knowledge of the spirit to our knowledge of nature in the Michael age, likewise we must add something to the achievements of the age of Gabriel in the technological field. In the Michael age, technology becomes magical because it reaches into subsensible realms; in order to maintain a balance, therefore, religious life must also become magical.

We must take a step towards a new Reformation. Religious life must be raised from the paucity of the intellectual age to the level of spiritual substance. The meaning of religion must once again be that spiritual powers are ready to help us if only we would call on them. We must find a direct connection to these divine forces, and especially to those we indicate with the name of Christ. If this succeeds, we will establish balance, and technology will be able to progress without interruption. After all, we cannot do without it. We cannot turn back the clock; we must move forward.

The technological age has built machines, and we will continue to build machines, but in the age of Michael we must build altars as well. It will then be revealed that not only the powers of the abyss but also those of the Christ being have approached the gates of the earthly world. All that is needed are courageous people who dare to break through the thin wall. In the age of Gabriel, it was human cleverness that mattered: cleverness and intelligence that gave rise to science and technology. But it was the kind of intelligence that ran under its own power, and that humanity could develop without becoming morally different. What is needed now must be drawn out of our innermost being. In the Michael age, it is not cleverness but courage of heart that counts, for what causes people to doubt a supersensible world is unconscious cowardice and inner timidity. We must shake that off.

Gabriel was, and still is, the power that guides people into birth because he always leads from the spiritual into the earthly. He is involved when, in the womb, a bodily sheath is prepared for the incarnating human soul. That is why Gabriel's field of activity is that of heredity. For nearly four hundred years, it was appropriate to research the laws of heredity and gaze upon them with reverent eyes. However, continuing to emphasise the principles of heredity after the end of the Gabriel age is an anachronism. It can only arise from fanaticism because it no longer corresponds to the truth. In the age of Michael, it is not the bodily sheath in

5. THE MICHAEL AGE IN AUTUMN

which we live as human beings that matters, but the inner human being, who may need to throw off the bonds of heredity if they are to come into their own. This is the courage that must come to the fore in our spiritual attitude in the Michael age.

Heredity was Gabriel's concern. Freedom – that is, real, inner, practised spiritual initiative – is the concern of the Michael age. Only what we create out of true freedom, out of the spirit, is constructive. Communities that are based on blood relations will eventually disintegrate. Communities that we create and nurture out of the spirit, formed and built with patience, can become the nuclei of a new culture.

The feast day of Michael, September 29, falls at the beginning of the autumn. The season is itself a sublime parable for the spirit of our age. Just when the fruit is ripening on trees and bushes and the harvest is imminent, we must learn to look at it not just from the human perspective, the recipients of nature's gifts, but also from the perspective of nature.

In nature, fruit that has ripened over the course of the year is cast off and dropped. What people do with it is not what nature primarily cares about. It is shed. And when the leaves turn golden afterwards, the ruthless spirit goes around again and does not rest until the last leaf has fallen from the bare trees. What does the spirit of autumn want? It wants to cast out the old so that there is room for the new.

What we experience year after year in nature as a matter of course, we experience today in unique grandeur in our culture. We have lived long enough on the magnificent monuments of the past. Parents have shown their children the fountain on Römerplatz in Frankfurt, around which great coronation festivals were celebrated, or the houses of Hans Sachs and Albrecht Dürer in the old Nuremberg streets. Many have felt strengthened by the sight of the Romanesque churches and Gothic cathedrals. But how easily have people allowed their reliance on the past to dissuade them from producing something new that corresponds precisely with the present moment. Now, the ruthless spirit of the age is smashing the monuments of the past, causing many people to ask themselves, 'What are we now to pass on to the younger generation as a legacy of culture?'

Increasingly, we will be compelled to create culture purely from within without relying on the values of earlier times. This is the Archangel Michael speaking to us, breaking down the old pillars to make room for the new. But the new does not emerge on its own.

The Archangel Gabriel was the preserving power. During his rulership it was in keeping with the spirit of the times that people collected old things in museums and elsewhere. Michael, however, is the advancing power who wants to promote human beings. But we are not advanced by remaining comfortable in the earthly world. A person can be successful in the bourgeois sense. They can have everything on earth that their heart desires, and yet, when they pass through the gate of death, they can stand there as an utterly impoverished and undeveloped soul. That is the danger people face. They can all too easily stand still in life and find themselves in the same spot at sixty or seventy as when they were twenty-one. They have learnt nothing new and have spent their time repeating the same things, making only slight modifications. Life thus feels empty and without meaning.

Today, we can arrive at the view that those who have lost much are favoured over those who, whether by destiny or cleverness, still have everything. Yet those who have been struck by destiny have been advanced inwardly. Many people have crossed the threshold and been jolted in their eternal being by the bitter, cruel suffering of our time.

People used to think that misfortune was a form of punishment. Today, we must learn that the more human history advances, the more misfortune can also help to chisel out the eternal human essence from the raw material of earthly existence. The old saying, 'The Lord chastises those whom he loves' (Heb. 12:6), only needs to be modified slightly. Whoever God strikes is one from whom he wants something. God's loving ray of light falls on us, no matter how different it looks from the outside. Those spared by destiny may ask themselves whether that is perhaps because they are of no interest or importance to the higher world. Or perhaps they are not yet able to join the ranks of the bearers of destiny through loss and sacrifice.

In the Michael age we must learn to think more broadly. If Germany and its people are now lying on the ground, we could

5. THE MICHAEL AGE IN AUTUMN

perhaps see it as a sign that something should and indeed can emerge from Central Europe again. Where should the ideas come from that the world needs today if not from the long-suffering soil of Central Europe? The Bible says, 'What good is it for someone to gain the whole world, yet forfeit their soul?' (Mark 8:36). Today, we can turn that around and say, 'What harm can it do a person if they lose the whole world and yet in so doing find themselves?'

The Archangel Michael is strict. He causes the cracks in our world to appear, but only because he wants to pull down the wall that separates us from the world of the spirit. We are supposed to look through them and perceive the light of divine love shining through the outer barrier. That is what we mean at the altars of The Christian Community when, during Michaelmas, we say that the earnestness of Michael stands before the gentleness of Christ. When we break through the crumbling wall of the sensory world and enter the spiritual world beyond, we become calm and confident because we know again why we are alive.

Two thousand years ago the voice of John the Baptist rang out to prepare the first coming of Christ: 'Change your heart and mind! The axe has already been laid at the root of the trees.'

That call also resounds today, but not in words. The one who speaks those words today is the Archangel Michael, who is preparing Christ's second coming. The catastrophic collapses we see around us are an urgent call for people to penetrate the veil that separates us from the approaching spiritual world and the sun of Christ.

We can learn much from the previous Michael age, which unfolded between the seventh and the third centuries BC: military cataclysms dominated that time, great empires arose and fell, and there was no end to the storms of war. Will our age also take such a course now that we have two wars behind us? Will we also see many more empires rise and fall?

Yet the previous Michael age had another aspect. It was a time in which many spiritual messengers appeared, for in such an age, God does not leave people alone. Individuals break through and bring down from the heavens what is needed to plant something new. Even in our age, we will not be left alone; there will be people working among us who will courageously bring down from the heavens what we need for the earth. If you would hear it, one such person has already worked among us: Rudolf Steiner. His work has provided us with ideas that we can build on not just for decades but for hundreds of years to come.

The previous Michael age led humans to awaken to the ego and become independent personalities. Today's Michael age should lead ego-endowed human beings to awaken to the spirit and learn to grasp the spirit. Today, we are to awaken to the world in which Christ is. If there are great leaders in our age, one thing will be unmistakable, and that is whether they work for themselves or are forerunners of Christ. Rudolf Steiner was a great proclaimer of Christ. His achievement was, above all, to help us better understand Christianity and, through the knowledge of Christ he brought, to find the key to life on earth.

On the path through the present Michael age, rich in destinies and struggles, the person who knows where the hand on the World Clock is today will pause again and again in their work. Instead of chiselling away at the world – which they must do as best they can – they will feel that they are themselves are the raw material on which an invisible sculptor is setting their chisel. That is what Michelangelo did in the Sistine Chapel, as Conrad Ferdinand Meyer tells us. There we see the titanic creator resting his chisel, and turning to the deity he says:

> You moulded the first human from clay.
> I am already made of harder stuff,
> Master, you'll need your hammer ready.
> Sculptor God, strike! I am the stone.

6

The Confrontation with Evil
(1947)

Those who adhere to Schiller's words, 'The world's history is the world's judgement', can feel called to freedom and participation in service of the good.[1] By contrast, the idea of the 'Last Judgement' appeals to our fear and not to our sense of freedom. It has its roots in the Old Testament and places humanity under an inescapable decision imposed from the hereafter. More than is admitted in traditional devotional circles, it has contributed to holding human beings back in their development, keeping them at an immature stage.

We misunderstand the writings of the New Testament if we believe we can derive from them the imagery usually associated with the Last Judgement. For example, when we read in the great resurrection chapter of Paul's first epistle to the Corinthians, 'For the trumpet will sound, the dead will be raised imperishable, and we will be changed' (1Cor. 15:51f), we should read this in an apocalyptic sense. It does not mean that graves will open as if by some monstrous miracle, and that the great reckoning will take place for those who ascend from them. If we think in this way then we remain stuck in a petty, moralising way of seeing things that is more in accord with an Old Testament view. When Paul speaks of the last trumpet, he does not mean to use a motif of terror to awaken fear of a judgemental deity in the hearts of his readers. He uses the same precise, pictorial vocabulary drawn from the same apocalyptic vision that John employs in his Revelation. The Apocalypse allows us to recognise that the 'last trumpet' concludes only one of many aeonic rounds that the destiny of our world must undergo.

After the seven trumpets have sounded, world history and world judgement continue. The temple in heaven opens, from which the seven golden bowls are brought forth. As they are poured out, the trials that have already come upon humanity in the round of the trumpets will increase on the earth. If we learn to read the apocalyptic language, freed from rigid dogma and egoistical religious concepts, then monumental perspectives open up to us when we search for parallels between John's Revelation and what Paul describes as the content of the seventh trumpet. Paul's message speaks of the great storm of transformation that will one day pass through humanity. In the midst of life there is death and resurrection as the luminous world of the spirit rescues corruptible being from its demise. The Revelation to John shows us the confrontation with the forces of evil as the content of the seventh trumpet. Michael's battle with the dragon takes place and humanity has to pass the tests that the beast from the abyss prepares for it. Today, we are in the midst of a world history that is also a world judgement to a remarkable degree. Our spirits can hear the seventh trumpet sounding. The confrontation with evil is perhaps the most topical task there is.

Michael's battle with the dragon takes place in heaven. The Archangel is victorious and throws the conquered dragon down onto the earth. But what does that mean? Are we to imagine that demonic forces were originally fellow inhabitants of heaven?

Again, habitual, narrow-minded ideas about heaven and hell, with God in his heaven and Satan in hell, get in the way. But that is not how the Bible thinks. We do not have a supersensible world above us and another far below us. We are right in the middle of it. We are neighbours of supersensible powers at every turn, both the inspiring spirits who protect and promote us and those who want to corrupt us. Today we already have sufficient experience that we are closer to them, especially to hell. We may not yet be able to speak of heaven in the same way, although we are just as close to it.

For now, let us stick to the motif that the demonic powers are also fellow inhabitants of heaven. We can refer to the Book of Job as the biblical Faust poem. It begins with a dialogue between the Lord God and Satan regarding Job:

> One day the angels came to present themselves before the Lord, and Satan also came with them. The Lord said to Satan, 'Where have you come from?' Satan answered the Lord, 'From roaming throughout the earth, going back

6. THE CONFRONTATION WITH EVIL

and forth on it.' Then the Lord said to Satan, 'Have you considered my servant Job? There is no one on earth like him; he is blameless and upright, a man who fears God and shuns evil.' (Job 1:6–8)

Of course, the adversary knows Job and asks God for permission to tempt and torment him. God gives the devil free rein: just try it, he says, you will not succeed! We realise with amazement that God has faith in human beings.

Goethe picked up on that in his Faust tragedy, in the prologue in Heaven. First the sons of God appear, the archangels Raphael, Gabriel and Michael, and then Mephistopheles. A similar conversation ensues between him and God, with the Lord giving Mephisto permission to tempt Faust to the best of his ability:

> THE LORD: Let it be so: to you is given the power
> That may seduce this soul from his true source,
> And drag him down with you, in fatal hour,
> If you can wholly bend him to your force.
> But stand ashamed when called on to confess:
> A good man in his dark, bewildered course
> Will not forget the way of righteousness.[2]

The Lord God, believing in human beings, predicts that the devil will fail. Here, the character of Faust as portrayed by Goethe is more Christian than we normally hear from many pulpits, usually inspired by the more straightforward morality of a man who sells his soul to the devil. Goethe's *Faust* in this respect is a more modern-day, poetic retelling of the Book of Job, which itself, in the apocalyptic style of its writing, can be seen as a sister scripture to John's Revelation.

In both the Book of Job and Goethe's *Faust*, the tempting power is initially in heaven. It is given permission to cause a person on earth every difficulty and to lure him into the abyss. With the consent and will of God, the human being has to deal with evil. This is the attitude that a contemporary Christianity should bring to people.

In Chapter 12 of the Apocalypse, at the sound of the seventh trumpet, Michael's victory over the dragon leads to the adversary being thrown down upon the earth. It is the will of divine spirits that we battle demonic powers. Why? Because the angelic realms believe in us. It is not as if we could remain undefiled in our confrontations with the powers of the abyss. We must pass through many abysses. And yet we can still prevail. Thus, the confrontation with evil, which also runs through our age, is the direct continuation of a battle that has already taken place in heaven. Michael's battle with the dragon merges into the battle that human beings must now fight.

It has long been a great inner help to many people to know that we are currently living in a Michael age. This realisation has protected them from falling prey to all kinds of illusions. They understand and see through what is going on around them.

In the cyclic succession of archangels who ascend from the task of folk spirit to that of time spirit, it is today again the turn of the sun Archangel Michael, the archangel of Christ himself. What character must earthly history then assume? Michael's battle against the forces of the dragon in the supersensible world always introduces a Michael age. Such a victory in heaven also occurred at the beginning of the current archangel age, in which we have lived since the last quarter of the nineteenth century. The result is that since then, demons have been unleashed upon the earth and humanity has had to deal with the forces of evil to an ever-increasing extent. If there are wars and catastrophes on earth, it is because people do not realise that they are confronted with invisible opponents they must fight and overcome. Anyone who consciously feels connected to the Michael age, to whom the image of the archangel guiding the destinies of the present day speaks, can at the same time have the comforting certainty: the demonic forces that are turning our age upside down have already been defeated. No matter how insurmountable they may seem, they would not be here to oppress us if they had not first been cast down from heaven to earth. They are enemies with broken wings. It is not presumptuous for humanity to muster the courage – however small and insignificant it may feel – to take up the fight with inner strength.

The more apocalyptic the times become and the more we recognise that the Revelation to John is an outline and spiritual mirror

6. THE CONFRONTATION WITH EVIL

of the destiny of the present, the more clearly Christianity will take on a Michaelic character. It is the signature feature of our time that evil emerges openly. For that reason, it is important that we do not cling to medieval, superstitious ideas about the devil. Today, people lack the right concepts that will enable them to recognise and understand the times we are living in.

People are living with demonic powers and yet are completely lacking the spiritual wisdom necessary to oppose them. Good alone will not get us a single step further, and we must consider the reasons for that very carefully. We sense that demonic forces have been unleashed upon humanity. When the guns fell silent in 1945, it was fashionable to talk about demons. Indeed, there was hardly a magazine that didn't talk about them. Pastors preached about demons from the pulpit and professors said from their lecterns, 'We have faced demons.' But this remains only so much talk if we do not feel obliged to fundamentally revise our worldview. After all, it is woefully inconsistent to start talking about devils and demons while claiming to be a modern person who thinks in a way that denies the existence of a supersensible world. Where is there space in the conventional scientific view for the demons that people suddenly seem to believe in again? Talk of demons cannot be taken seriously because it does not arise from a clear, consistent way of thinking. It is true that we have looked the demons in the eye, but it is unacceptable to believe that we can talk about demons while continuing to think that there is no supersensible world. We must recognise that the materialistic-scientific worldview has long since gone bankrupt. It has been refuted, if not by good divinities, then at least by demons.

When it comes to our knowledge, the greatest obstacle to penetrating the forces of evil is our dualistic thinking: our view of heaven and hell, of good and evil, as two factors that are opposed to each other. We think that if we side with good by doing good deeds, then we will be able to deal with evil. But it is not like that.

We have experienced enough revelations of the demonic to say that human beings have become animals: the beast has revealed itself through people. The demons of an animalistic brutality have appeared on the scene and efforts are underway to bring those who have succumbed to this seduction to justice. That must happen, of course. But we should also recognise something else. There is not simply a demonic, animalistic brutality, which has risen to such unmistakable heights (or perhaps that should be plumbed such abominable depths), but also a theory of the human animal that is less easy to see through and which dominates the entire cognitive life of humanity.

We have a scientific view that understands human beings only insofar as they belong to the animal kingdom. There is no true anthropology. For example – and this happens just as well today as it did at the time of National Socialism – one proclaims a theory of heredity according to which human beings, like animals, are the product of hereditary and environmental influences. One has the animal in one's thinking, even if one is not guilty of any brutality. What are the likely consequences of a thinking that categorises human beings as animals? Might it not be that it becomes true? The thoughts we have about humanity ultimately influence and shape us. If we understand human beings according to experiments carried out on rabbits, mice and other animals, then we should not be surprised if an animalistic mentality breaks through.

Evil appears not only in the field of will, but also in the field of thought and cognition. But it does not immediately make itself apparent there. For example, if someone tortures or kills the person next to them, their bestial mentality is not difficult to diagnose. But when a scholar writes a book that claims to be highly scientific, it is not so easy to realise that this could also be demonic. There may even be a much more demonic danger here than where inhumanities are directly committed.

What means does Mephistopheles use to bring Faust down once he has received permission from God? Early on, in the first part, he prompts Faust to incur guilt in his relationship with Gretchen, but that is not the only thing. Later, at the beginning of the second part, Mephistopheles makes a witty appearance at the imperial court, where he counsels a remedy for the distress the empire has fallen into. He appears as the ingenious inventor of paper money that will remedy all misery.[3]

Here we come face to face with one of Goethe's most important cultural prophecies. At that time, paper money had only recently appeared in Europe. Since then, we have become thor-

6. THE CONFRONTATION WITH EVIL

oughly familiar with the problems it causes. But do people today agree with Goethe that paper money came from Mephistopheles?

We have not yet fully seen through the forces of evil. During the nineteenth century, many of Mephistopheles' ideas took root among humanity – it was the only way that most modern technological achievements could be developed. However, temptation is also at play here. Rudolf Steiner has pointed out how Goethe personified the forces of evil in the figure of Mephistopheles, but that he could not properly distinguish the two aspects of the demonic. As a result, Mephisto is both the devil and Satan, as the Bible says, or Lucifer and Ahriman, as anthroposophy refers to them. On the one hand, demonic powers act in an intoxicating and seductive manner, and on the other in a cool and clever soulless way. Goethe combined these hot and cold adversaries in Mephistopheles because he could not make a clear distinction between them.

In John's Revelation, evil initially appears in the form of a single dragon, but then it divides into two beasts (Chapter 13). The dragon felled by Michael rises again from the abyss in two forms. From the sea there arises a beast with seven heads and ten horns, and on land there appears a two-horned beast in the likeness of a lamb.

Awareness of the dual form of evil is an essential apocalyptic key. The image of the two beasts was still well known everywhere in the ancient world. For example, the Book of Enoch, an ancient Jewish apocalyptic scripture, describes the two beasts from the abyss in detail. The monster rising from the sea is called Leviathan and the two-horned beast that emerges from the ground is Behemoth. Furthermore, in the Book of Job, Job's trials culminate in an encounter with this double countenance of evil. Of Leviathan, God says:

> Flames stream from its mouth; sparks of fire shoot out.
> Smoke pours from its nostrils as from a boiling pot over
> burning reeds. Its breath sets coals ablaze. (Job 41:19–21)

This is the Luciferic power, which brings human passions to the boil. It inspires ambition and all vain illusions that tear us from the earth. It consumes the soul and makes it weak. Those who surrender to this power of arrogance and selfishness will be called Leviathan.

> Its chest is hard as rock, hard as a lower millstone. When it rises up, the mighty are terrified; they retreat before its thrashing. (Job 41:24f)

People are only ever vain or power-hungry or autocratic out of weakness and hidden fear; they inflate themselves because they are not strong in heart. Those who have inner strength, however, are quiet and modest.

Job also encounters the two-horned beast:

> Look at Behemoth ... What strength it has in its loins, what power in the muscles of its belly! Its tail sways like a cedar; the sinews of its thighs are close-knit. Its bones are tubes of bronze, its limbs like rods of iron. (Job 40:15–18)

This cold adversary is described as a crushing machine. Job, the Old Testament Faust, in enduring his trials justifies the trust of the deity who allowed the evil power to tempt him. The sting of evil is removed through the victorious powers of his heart. It can now be said of Satan-Behemoth, 'It ranks first among the works of God' (Job 40:19). The encounter with him means that Job has reached the threshold of the spiritual world and he can now say to God: 'My ears had heard of you, but now my eyes have seen you' (Job 42:5).

This threshold scene pervades all ancient mythologies. Thus we see in Homer's *Odyssey*, where Odysseus has to sail through the Strait of Messina and pass between Scylla and Charybdis, a six-headed monster on one side of the strait who snatches sailors from passing ships, and a sea monster that churns up the sea and swallows ships whole.[4] But this is more than just a strait with whirlpools and monsters. Scylla and Charybdis are also the two beasts that emerge from the abyss: Scylla from solid land, Charybdis from the sea. The Edda, the apocalypse of Old Norse mythology, depicts the two spawns of the underworld as the Midgard Serpent, which sets everything on fire with its fiery

6. THE CONFRONTATION WITH EVIL

breath, creating the world conflagration known as Muspilli, and Fenris Wolf, the cold, ravening beast that ultimately kills even Odin, the father of the gods.

Knowledge of the dual aspect of evil provides us with a key to the problems of our immediate present. The beast with the seven heads and ten horns that rises from the sea is an adversarial power that human beings must fight within themselves. We are confronted by Leviathan, or Lucifer, who rises from the depths of the unconscious, threatening to overwhelm us with a flood of emotion, turning us into mindless souls adrift from the sure guidance of the spirit. All moral aberrations are caused by a person's soul not being under the direction of their true spiritual ego. When considering the nature of evil, we usually focus on this opposing force: moral evil.

The other two-horned beast, however, has been far too little recognised. It rises from the solid land, meaning it comes to us from earthly things. It mingles with natural science and technology, with humanity's endeavours to understand and master the earthly world. Behemoth, or Ahriman, rises from the midst of earthly realities and wants to seduce humans with a soulless intellectuality. The intellectuality that invents paper money and builds machines brings this danger with it, and we have come to know its effects to a horrific extent. Certainly, we cannot do without technology. But the Ahrimanic power has triumphed over humanity. We developed technology with an insatiable hunger without developing ourselves along with it. Now humanity stands helpless and enslaved, tyrannised by the machinery and the bureaucracy it has created. We must realise that we can only progress in a free and proper way if we develop inwardly as much as have outwardly. Everything around us is collapsing because the rapid development of civilisation has taken the path of soulless intellectuality, of mere cleverness. We have not noticed that this is just as much a demonic aberration as that of immorality. Alongside moral and personal evil, therefore, there is objective and social evil.

When will we begin to demand accountability and seek balance and healing? People are right to demand justice for the terrible crimes that have been committed. But how can the power that has hollowed out souls, namely the mindset of the materialistic era, be banished? The power of evil that is decisive for our time is at work in the materialistic worldview. We have taken it for granted as the basis of life, even in our churches.

In earlier times, humanity had more to do with Lucifer, but we have now entered a time in which the confrontation with Ahriman must occur. How will that be accomplished? Through the liberation of thought from soullessness and mere capriciousness, and through the struggle for a fully human, spiritually correct way of thinking and perceiving. In that respect, Rudolf Steiner's life work represents a Michaelic achievement of the highest rank, a militant accomplishment through which the errors of the materialistic worldview have been overcome. For a worldview that does not include the supersensible world and, above all, does not believe that human beings are supersensible beings is a lie. Science may well be right in some respects and has indeed produced impressive results. It would be foolish to deny that hereditary research or modern atomic physics have made the most phenomenal discoveries. But all of that becomes a lie if we think that this is all there is and do not recognise that we are only poking around on the outside of existence. We all carry a lot of hereditary material, yet we must not think that we are only this material. We must recognise that the true essence of the human being, the spiritual human being, transcends heredity and is merely housed in its inherited physical body. If we do not add supersensible knowledge to our current view of the world, then even the most brilliant science becomes a lie and a falsification of life.

In grand style, Ahriman has succeeded in making people believe the physical world is the whole world. Souls have been made insensitive and morally weak through these cold demons that have crept unnoticed into the human condition. It is no wonder that Lucifer also finds rich prey to harvest in the footsteps of Ahriman. Mere external knowledge has caused the conscience to die. Within the tremendous machine-like systems into which social existence has been forced according to the principles of technology – 'the totalitarian state', 'total warfare' – human life has lost its value. People did not even realise how social life was being brutally destroyed.

6. THE CONFRONTATION WITH EVIL

If we take seriously the dual nature of evil as presented to us in the thirteenth chapter of the Apocalypse, we realise how misleading traditional dualistic thinking is, which merely contrasts good and evil. Evil is not opposed by the good, but by *another* evil. And where do we find the good? We find it in the idea of the golden mean as formulated in Greek ethics, in the balance between the extremes of the two opposing forces. That is why the Archangel Michael holds the balance scales in his hand. The golden mean is more than just a glib maxim. It is the key to the mysteries of morality.

We must allow ourselves to be served by Lucifer, without whom we would have no artistic ability, no art, and we must also allow ourselves to be served by Ahriman, because we need science and technology. But human beings must stand in the centre and keep the beasts from the abyss in check on both sides. We can only solve the riddle of evil through a trinitarian way of thinking. Although still wholly undeciphered, the mystery of the divine Trinity solves all riddles of existence for us, including that of evil. What power stands in the centre and allows us to find our way between the devil and Satan, between Lucifer and Ahriman? At the centre is the sun spirit, the golden heart of the world, Christ himself. Michael is the archangel of the sun and of Christ because, as the servant of the golden equilibrium, he helps to overcome the demons.

What is meant by the ten horns of the seven-headed Leviathan that rises from the sea? Why does this beast have more horns than heads? Its tendency toward hardening indicates that the Luciferic danger suggests holding on to past contents and forces. Humanity must be progressive and move with the times. But we must not go to the other extreme and be so progressive that our souls cannot keep up. The two-horned beast is described as performing miracles. For example, it makes fire fall from the sky. The whole of modern technology consists of miracles insofar as it works with electricity and now also with atomic energy. Such forces are not 'of this world'. However, the source of these forces is not the supersensible world but the subsensible world: the abyss. Yet we do not realise this.

The end of Chapter 13 of the Apocalypse states that the number of the two-horned beast is 666. Primitive interpretations that say this number refers to the Emperor Nero, for example, fall far short of their grasp of what is meant here. In the monumental breadth of vision of the Apocalypse, the number 666 signifies an exciting moment in world evolution. We must understand it in the rhythms of a base-seven system of counting, in which six always marks the end before the start of a larger unit, a new round. Thus, 666 is like 999 in our counting system, the one before one thousand. It captures the moment before development achieves a new level of completion.

Why is 666 the number of Ahriman, the two-horned beast? Because it is the Ahrimanic power that exaggerates progress. It is always crying, 'Make haste! Make haste!' People are frightened, and that is how the whole rush of modern life comes about. But in the rush they miss out on something important, which is that some things need to be cultivated in stillness and silence; they require time and patience to come to fruition. But that is impossible if you are always on the go. The fact that 666 is the number of Ahriman means that wherever he is working, he is constantly cracking the whip and demanding that we make haste.

Nowadays, people are often busybodies without a whip being cracked because they no longer have the strength of inner calm. That is how weak souls have already become. The world of Ahrimanic civilisation, which rushes everything, inventing the belief in busyness, hollows out our souls and makes them inwardly unstable. The only way to defend oneself against that danger is through systematically cultivating inwardness, devotion and focus. That is the mission of the renewed sacramental life, as it is cultivated in The Christian Community. We learn to take time in front of the altar and free ourselves from the harrying influence of the number 666. Then the Millennial Kingdom is not something to be established in the outer world, but instead something to be found within through the practice of contemplation. A person can be morally impeccable and an outstanding member of human society yet still be incapable of solitude and stillness. Despite their impressive busyness, they are pitifully weak and in danger of giving up their humanity.

We are thus caught between two extremes: on the one hand, clinging to the past, unable to separate ourselves from what we have merely brought with us, and on the other, the number 666

6. THE CONFRONTATION WITH EVIL

that plagues us with hurry. Yet between them lies the golden mean that is the sphere of true devotion. Especially those who work with machines or electricity must know that they need inner balance in the face of the depletion to which they are exposed. But how can a modern person find a balance if they think they can manage without piety?

Today, we must find the path to a kind of devoutness that modern humans can once again cultivate honestly. It is the religion of resting in the golden middle, in the sphere of Christ, which is also the sphere of Michael. Although it seems paradoxical, cultivating peace is also the most effective way of fighting evil. If one wants to survive the battle of the spirits, one doesn't always have to be so combative. From a soul filled with peace, which we gain through devotion and piety in the sacramental sense, a new morality emerges. We can again fulfil what we have the will to do and not fall short of our intentions. Souls have become weak through Ahriman; through devotion, they become strong again. This is the battle we must fight today.

Before the Revelation to John describes Michael's battle with the dragon, it says in the last verse of Chapter 11, 'Then God's temple in heaven was opened, and within his temple was seen the ark of his covenant.' The battles that achieve victory over the forces of evil occur in front of the altar of the open temple. With the world of the altar as a backdrop, we too can confront the adversarial powers and overcome them.

7

Europe's Inspiring Spirit
(1947)

Is the crisis into which Europe has fallen today a trial to be endured and passed or the final death throes of a civilisation? When Europe was born as the daughter of the ancient world, the same guiding spirit of the ages presided over the advancing human race as it does today. In the round of archangels who rise in succession to the level of time spirit, or zeitgeist, it is Michael, the archangel of the sun, who is at the helm of development today. Under thunderous skies reddened by conflagration, a twilight of the gods has broken over Europe.

Europe was born when the light of human thought shone from the foreheads of the Greek thinkers. When the ancient wisdom of the gods and the spirituality of the great Asian mother continent were translated into human thought, the daughter continent began to develop a life of its own. Whereas in Asia, the primeval tranquillity of the laws of duration still held sway with their endlessly repeating cycles of time, in Europe, time's arrow now took flight. Under the spiritual patronage of the stern, forward-striving Archangel Michael, the early Greek philosophers transformed the timeless ideas of the gods of ancient wisdom into enthusiastic, action-bearing human thinking. It is true that Pythagoras, like Plato, returned to Asia and Egypt to sit at the feet of wise teachers, as did other sons of the Michael age, such as the Hebrew prophets, but what they learned there through profound spiritual experience, they transformed into human thoughts.

Towards the end of that Michael age, Alexander the Great, the young Macedonian king and student of Aristotle, brought back to Asia what Europe had made of her original gift. All previous spiritual life had been characterised by the sentence *ex oriente lux*: from the East comes light, meaning the light of the primordial wisdom that had lit the torch of human thought. Now, in

7. EUROPE'S INSPIRING SPIRIT

Alexander's marches, the light of human thought from the West responded to the wellsprings of the gods to whom it owed its life: *ex occidente lux* – from the West comes light – emerged for the first time.

Just as Greece developed the dawning light of thought, so Rome cultivated the vestal fire of human will to shape the earth. When the Christian stream entered the world, it initially followed the old law of *ex oriente lux*. From the Asian coastal strip overlooking Europe, Christianity spread mainly westwards, pouring into the still-young European world. The people of the Old Testament, dwelling on the margins of Asia, had prepared the earthly body for Christ; the Greeks, with their wisdom-infused thinking, could understand Christ, and the Romans through the instrument of their humanity and the power of their will, were able to become Christian.

Like the gospels, the miracle of early Christian theology made full use of Greek thought and language. Michael, the archangel of the sun, had inspired the Greek thinkers and poets so that before the cradle of Christianity, Europe could offer up a human thinking that was still illuminated by the spirit.

When the first three centuries of Christian life were over, the phase of European development borne by the Greeks and Romans also ended. Then came the great Migration Period as huge numbers of people migrated south from northern and northeastern Europe. They brought with them the legacy of an ancient Germanic-Celtic wisdom, which mixed in the Roman Empire with what had become of the Greek thought inspired by Michael.

The Christian stream was briefly rejuvenated during this time, having become ecclesiastically rigid by adapting to the ageing Roman world. Waves of a more primitive Nordic Christianity swept through the lands, but before they, too, succumbed to the rigidifying influence, they were able to plant in the soil of Western Europe the seed of Grail Christianity from which a cosmic Christian wisdom radiates. As during the reign of Alexander, though much more quietly this time, a light shone from the West to the East. It was another youthful response to the ancient gifts of wisdom that Mother Asia had given to Europe. However, this second wave of early Christianity could only keep itself alive by fighting. If it had maintained its gentle, quiet splendour, it would not have been able to stand up to the increasingly powerful and earthly Church stream.

The image of the Archangel Michael played a significant role among the people who adopted Christianity during and after the Migration Period, right up to the time of the Crusades when the new empires of the Goths and the Lombards were formed on Greek and Roman soil. Enthusiasm, courage and heroism were ignited everywhere by the thought of the archangel. Under the banner of Michael, there was a struggle for a Christianity that was free from ecclesiastical rigidities and papal paternalism. In his image, the tribes and peoples who were the bearers of the rejuvenated Europe saw a spiritual ideal calling to them from the future. As far as they were concerned, Michael was Europe's inspiring spirit, and under his sign the newly Christian continent's mission would be fulfilled.

Europe subsequently matured and entered its adulthood. Until then, the thoughts conceived on its soil had focussed more on the heavenly world than on the world of the senses; images taken from the ancient myths or from the mysteries of Christianity still flowed into them. Now, the human spirit took hold of the sensory world with all the joy of discovery. An earthly culture was born in which the supersensible world, hitherto experienced as a dream, was extinguished, and thinking, now perceived as the soul's own activity, set about trying to understand and master the outer world. The age of discoveries and inventions had dawned, and with it the beginnings of modern science and technology quickly appeared on the scene. The richness of the sensory world cast such a spell over human beings that they forgot the spiritual spheres. The experience of freedom associated with thinking had set the human spirit in motion and humanity no longer appreciated divine guidance.

It is part of humanity's destiny on the grandest scale that Europe's discovery of America is one of the conquests that made human beings masters of the earth. Europe's relationship with the world fundamentally changed as a result. The duality between the original mother, Asia, and her daughter, Europe, was transformed in a mysterious way into a triad. Europe still felt the great womb of its life in the East, but the gigantic enigma of the

7. EUROPE'S INSPIRING SPIRIT

West became increasingly important to her. America fascinated Europe to such an extent that it ignited a tremendous acceleration of science and technology. Whereas twinges of homesickness for a lost paradise in the East still afflicted Europe, America signalled the danger of bringing about too early what was only meant to be fully developed in the future. Humanity could not keep pace in developing its spiritual powers.

Meanwhile, Central Europe was beginning to awaken to itself. The genuine life of the European soul flowed alongside the more extreme soullessness of the materialistic worldview and blossomed in the intellectual life of all its peoples. There was always a remembrance of Greece's early days as the spirit of the previous Michael age inspired the true geniuses of Europe, such as Goethe, in their creations. After Goethe's death, twilight fell quickly over Europe, ultimately leading to the great catastrophic collapses of our time. But what struggles to survive among the shattered ruins is not the true Europe but a distorted one. By allowing itself to be driven to the extremes of Western materialism, Central Europe had become unfaithful to itself and to its task of holding the balance between East and West. In light of this, one could tentatively ask if the present crisis might not serve to lead Europe back to its true spiritual destiny by liberating it from all that is false in our external civilisation.

Alongside the rise of the scientific worldview and the development of technology and the modern monetary system, a new tendency arose in human society: nationalism. Before this time, there had been a more general European life that was broadly similar. Now, individual peoples with a national character began to crystallise, and people started to take pride in their own national identity. However, the fact that humanity was losing sight of the spirit so rapidly meant that there were also profound shadows and dangers.

Individuals fall prey to egotism when, instead of remaining conscious of their supersensible nature, they become more earthly. This danger was matched by a national egotism that set the emerging nation-states against each other, and a technology that ultimately provided a more complete means of a battle of all against all.

In the catastrophes of our time, just as technology is overtaking us, nationalism has increased. Due to increasing globalisation, a cosmopolitan wave is sweeping across the world. While there is much that is positive about this, we must be conscious of its negative aspects. The national peculiarities that came about as the result of European humanity individualising itself into distinct nations are in danger of being lost. In part, this is a result of the chaotic mixing of peoples that is occurring everywhere, and which brings with it a degree of resentment from local populations. Instead of the spiritual richness of colour in the interplay of peoples, all that remains are dividing lines between them.

This development is also a consequence of the fact that Europe is in danger of becoming unfaithful to itself. Europe is meant to use the free human ego's power of thought to ascend to the spiritual consciousness that the divine beings gave to a still unawakened, immature humanity in Asia. The dramatic and difficult destinies of the present age should and can serve this goal. In the work of Rudolf Steiner, the new Michaelic inspiration has begun to make a powerful impact, leading Europe forward on the path of its inner destiny, despite all its external downfalls. The lost balance between inner and outer can be restored. The scales of knowledge and achievement are no longer weighed down in favour of the outer world. Genuine spiritual knowledge begins to hold the balance against mere natural science, and the permeation of the spirit in all living conditions balances out the one-sidedness of technology. As the supersensible world opens up, humanity's spiritual horizon broadens, and we will no longer be inferior to the inventions and discoveries that marked the beginning of the modern age.

This also provides us with an astonishing view of a truly spiritual Europe. Some of the continent's peoples may be outwardly disempowered, but in spirit, they are no less alive because of this, perhaps even more so. Each individual human being is a supersensible entity, surrounded by their guiding angel. The nations that have emerged in Europe with their own national character are likewise, in their true essence, members of the spiritual world. Each is guided in its destiny by an actual being from the hierarchy of archangels. Over the shattered fields of our continent is the harmonious choir of the nations' guiding spirits,

7. EUROPE'S INSPIRING SPIRIT

organised in wonderful forms. If order is to radiate from somewhere into our chaotic outer life, it must come from that level and correspond with the harmonies that exist there.

However, the first thing that will reveal itself to the intuitive perception of larger numbers of people may not be the region of the archangels, but that of the spirit of our times. The Archangel Michael looks out over the areas where the apocalyptic destinies of our days have taken hold, light raying out from him in all directions. Below him, above the outwardly chaotic map of Europe, the divinely ordered ranks of the folk souls becomes recognisable. This is the positive aspect of the cosmopolitan procession that marches through our time. Europe is seen standing in the light of the archangel holding the scales in his hand as the true centre between East and West, establishing balance. Above him, the clouds break before the high spirit of the sun, whose countenance Michael is. From the sphere of Christ himself, light and strength will flow to a humanity devoid of ideas and strength.

The previous Michael age brought with it the birth of Europe. Michael's current work aims at a *rebirth* of Europe: that is, the resurrection of a spiritual Europe from the decline of its external balance of power. Under Michael's previous rule, the power of thought was born in human souls, replacing the sleeping, dreamlike beholding of the ancient world. Today, in the souls that have awakened through thinking and matured through difficult destinies, a visionary cognition is to be born. It emerges from the liberation and enhancement of an otherwise sense-bound, head-bound thinking. After the preparations humanity underwent in the previous Michael age, the Christ stream penetrated Europe from an earthly Holy Land. Today, after being spiritually channelled by the archangel of the age, Christ is to enter Europe from the Holy Land of the etheric world and from there into the whole of humanity.

8

The World Situation and the True Spirit of the Times

(1949)

The current world situation is not only becoming more urgent by the day, it is also becoming clear that what faces us is a religious problem. It is a fatal error to think that we are primarily dealing with emergencies and catastrophes in the economic or political fields. All difficulties in the outer spheres of life are nothing but the consequences of a fundamental spiritual crisis. The spiritual forces upon which humanity has lived until now are at an end, and we are witnessing the effects of this. We lack the creative ideas necessary for building new systems and productive cultural relationships, and much of what is happening now is governed by trial and error. Ideas are being asserted in such a fanatically one-sided way that confusion and collapse are only becoming more comprehensive.

But humanity today is not only bereft of good ideas; it has also been deserted by good spirits and we don't even know it. We are unaware of the sphere from which flow the forces and ideas that could help us immensely. Let us try to rise above our worm's-eye view, which only looks at the earth, and see how what is happening in our world today looks from a higher perspective.

The cataclysms that shook the old world order followed one another from the outbreak of the First World War. They were not isolated, large-scale disasters. There was a terrible consistency to them, with each one emerging as a consequence and an intensification of the one that came before it. As far as the external facts are concerned, we are on a consistent downward trend towards an actual ending of the world, and we have by no means reached the low point.

To understand the present moment, it is imperative to visualise the last three stages of this great landslide.

8. THE WORLD SITUATION

What happened in the 1930s could be described as a powerful vortex in the soul atmosphere of Central Europe. An emotional tornado of the greatest magnitude took hold of a world that appeared to be stable, but which had been shocked to the core by previous blows of destiny. Weighed and found too light, everything was thrown up into the air like scraps of paper. And in the fear, intoxication and monstrous megalomania of people, we saw only reflections and shadows of what was going on in the soul realm.

Chaos ensued in the second stage, spreading outwards as if in concentric waves. The European neighbourhood was affected first, the torch of war eerily illuminating the collapse of the previous world order. Then the waves spread around the entire globe, reaching even the most distant continents until, finally, no part of our planet was spared. People may be inclined to focus on local hardships and difficulties, but a proper understanding of what is happening is only possible if we look at the totality of chaos.

The third stage, which followed the vortex and chaos, can be described as the pull of the vacuum. In Central Europe, developments had been triggered by the spiritual and emotional tornado. An inner vacuum emerged that had long existed in secret and finally expressed itself in the rubble of German cities. Through the vortex, the extremes of both East and West fell into the vacuum and, without a centre to act as a buffer between them, collided catastrophically with each other. But what is it that meets in the centre from the East and the West?

Spirituality has always flowed westwards from the East. The old expression *ex oriente lux* – 'from the East, light' – indicates this. Even today, spirituality comes from the East. This may seem paradoxical, especially if we look to Russia. There we see how an idea was set in motion with fanatical vigour that in terms of content has nothing to do with religion; it is even hostile to the spirit. Yet just as all revolutionary movements in Russia during the time of the tsars were accompanied by messianic ideas of the end times, the idea of Communism as propagated by the East today is even more religiously fuelled, even though it appears virulently anti-religion. It is an extreme inversion of the idea of the kingdom of God and thus bears all the intensity of a religious conviction. The result is a magnificent one-sidedness.

Communism promotes prosperity for all, especially those belonging to the labouring classes, but if the opposite occurs, namely the impoverishment and suffering of the people, what happens then? Instead of correcting the idea, it is enforced all the more fanatically. This is because the idea is more important than the reality. The one-sidedness that we see coming from the East consists precisely in this: the violation of reality by the idea. But the violated reality, ultimately, is humanity.

From the West comes the opposite stream: a practical realism embodied in a branch of humanity gifted with the ability to organise external world affairs. But it is a realism that considers only the sense-perceptible world to be real and fails to recognise the spiritual world, the world of ideas, as the second half of reality. The result is the opposite one-sidedness: the violation of the idea by reality. But what kind of character does reality take on if we disregard everything idealistic? Chiefly, it is an economic one. From the West, people are threatened by an attitude that holds money and big business in high esteem. With the one-sidedness that comes from the East, we saw that the idea violates reality; in the West, however, it is reality that violates the idea. But which idea is it that is being violated? Once again it is humanity. We cannot understand human beings in their essence if we do not recognise that they are thinkers, the bearers of the world of ideas.

Bolshevism and capitalism are the catchwords with which the East and the West characterise each other and their mutual incompatibility. In and of themselves, such polarities could be highly fruitful and contribute to the richness of humanity's experience. Just as our globe has a North Pole and a South Pole, humanity could have an East Pole and a West Pole, spiritually speaking: one branch of humanity that is more spiritually oriented and one that is more worldly oriented. The fact that today the polarities are becoming dangerously one-sided and threatening to ignite new world wars in their sudden collision is not the fault of the East or the West. We are dealing here with the failure of the centre, hollowed out in soul and spirit, to unite the opposites and bring them into balance.

We find ourselves in the middle of an almost insoluble human conflict that the whole world fears will erupt in nuclear

8. THE WORLD SITUATION

conflagration. The extremes of East and West did not come up against real spiritual factors in the centre but were catastrophically sucked in by the vacuum that had been created. In the future, it will no longer be justified to call the Germans the thinkers and poets. How can the spiritual failure of humanity's centre be overcome? How can the spiritual realities that create equilibrium be made manifest when humanity is in danger of destroying itself through contradictions?

The clearer the diagnostic picture of the present moment, the more we must feel compelled to ask ourselves which spiritual powers are the directors of this monstrous drama. What real spirit of the times is making its will known here?

It is difficult to rise from the human level to that of the true spirit of the times. Goethe's Faust expresses his age's moving, destiny-shaping powers when he counters Wagner's witty comment on the spirit of the times: 'And what you call the Spirit of the Ages / is but the spirit of your learned sages.'[1]

If when we look for today's zeitgeist we stop at the spiritual forces that humanity brings forth from itself, then we can only speak of an 'un-spirit of the times'. All the turbulent and distressing conditions that have befallen humanity on earth result from some kind of un-spirituality: an un-spirituality that, under certain circumstances, reigns with an ingenious cleverness in all areas of life, not only in technology and economics, but also in art and religion. But there must be higher powers whose intentions are directly, or even indirectly, involved in the destiny of our times.

We can also put the question we face in terms of traditional religious life. What is God's attitude to what is happening on earth today? We have forgotten all too quickly that this question was asked by thousands of frightened people in bomb shelters during the air raids. People have tried to find an answer to that question in many ways. Some speak of the judgement of a wrathful God upon a godless humanity, but only those who have not yet broken free from the spell of the Old Testament can speak that way. The more Christianity comes to an understanding of its mysteries, the clearer it will be that the idea of an angry God does not belong in the New Testament, and that the words of John's letters – that God is love – belong to the fundamental truths of Christianity.

Without being aware of it, those who struggle to understand what is happening by asking how God can allow it are already touching on the mystery of the present in a more substantive way. Such a question only makes sense if we presuppose the existence of powers hostile to God and which God allows to exist for a time, just as he allows the devil to plague Job. Although the prevailing worldview has no room for it, the recognition of demonic powers runs through the spiritual life of our time in all possible forms.

However, it is at this point that our purely intellectual mode of thought fails us, and we must develop an apocalyptic imagination. One particular apocalyptic motif has played a repeated role in our time. It has been employed by megalomaniacs and cultural optimists, as well as in the religious materialism of certain American sects to express the imminent transformation of the earth into a paradise: it is the image of the Millennial Kingdom. How does the Bible itself present this imagination to us? Chapter 12 of the Revelation to John describes how a mighty angel descends from heaven, throws the demonic powers into the abyss and seals the abyss above them. For a thousand years, humanity then has peace from the powers of darkness and can pursue the fulfilment of its earthly tasks unhindered. At the end of the thousand years, the angel descends anew and opens the abyss again.

Understood apocalyptically, this event is something that happens again and again in the great rhythm of world history. We must also add that when the gates of hell are closed, the gates of heaven are likewise shut. Heaven will not open without the abyss being unsealed. Humanity cannot expect the help of the progressive spirits while being spared the temptations from the depths. Either there is peace from the tribulations of the abyss, in which case people will have to find their way without help from the heights, or the gates of the supersensible world are open upwards *and* downwards, in which case people must struggle for divine help in a battle with demonic forces. The sealing of the abyss by the angel of God, which thereby establishes the Millennial Kingdom, means that for a time humanity must develop what strength it can find within itself. The thousand years refers to a full round of historical development. When it occurs in the rhythm of development, the Millennial Kingdom expresses God's belief in

8. THE WORLD SITUATION

humanity's capacity for freedom. When the kingdom of demons is unleashed at the end of the thousand years, therefore, it is so that the soul powers humanity has developed in that time can be tested.

It should not be difficult to recognise where we stand today in this apocalyptic drama. The Millennial Kingdom is not ahead of us but behind us. Humanity has gone through a cycle of development in which it was left to its own devices from above and from below. That went so far that people finally lost sight of the existence of a supersensible world altogether.

We are now at the beginning of those world conditions that will occur when the angel has unsealed the abyss at the end of the thousand years. The powers of the abyss have already made themselves felt. But no matter how great the trials of the present and the near future will be, God's faith in humanity is revealed all the more powerfully after the end of God's great pause. God, who is love, trusts us to find our way amid the forces unleashed from the abyss and to do his work on earth.

The other motif contained in Chapter 12 of the Revelation to John is Michael's battle with the dragon, and this is in exact harmony with the motif of the Millennial Kingdom. Under the Archangel Michael's leadership, the victory of the sunlike spiritual powers is completed by overthrowing the spirits of darkness. But where is the dragon cast down? With a cry of woe, the Apocalypse reveals that the opposing powers are now unleashed on earth: 'Woe to the earth and the sea, because the devil has gone down to you!' (Rev. 12:12). But if the demons are loose on earth, this is not to torment or punish people. Instead, it is the cosmic consequence of a triumphant event that has taken place in the higher worlds. Humanity on earth is granted a kind of nobility by being trusted to bring the battle on earth to a victorious conclusion, which divine powers have already fought to a first victory in higher worlds. We can, therefore, recognise a Michael age as the time that follows an expired thousand-year kingdom. The storms of mighty spiritual battles rage through it. Only those who recognise that they are called upon and honoured to be co-warriors in a Michaelic battle can penetrate its true meaning.

Apocalyptic images that shed light on the riddles of our time are not only found in biblical books. Now and then a thinker or poet can interpret the signs of the times through such an image. There is a scene in Strindberg's *A Dream Play,* written shortly after 1900, in which we see a ship in extreme danger on the stormy sea, surrounded by thunder and lightning. The crew clings to the rigging and, in their fear, calls upon the help of Christ by singing the sea shanty, 'Christ, Kyrie, come to us across the sea.' A light breaks through the dark clouds and a luminous figure walks across the sea. The people on the ship are frightened by the light, and in their terror and confusion they throw themselves into the sea and drown. They do not realise that their prayer has been answered.

Even before the storm of the age had fully erupted, Strindberg had painted a picture of what is happening in humanity today. The approach of those powers that could bring help and salvation triggers downfalls because people are blind to the world from which that help comes. For example, when tremendous spiritual turmoil broke out in the 1930s, many felt that something new and unheard of was in the air. Yet in the age of materialism and intellectualism, the organs of the soul had become too deadened to recognise that the gates of a higher world had opened again and that a new revelation of Christ was imminent. People misinterpreted what was approaching in a crude, materialistic, political sense and threw themselves into the waves of the vortex without realising that they were committing themselves to destruction.

As never before, the supersensible world is breaking in with force and abundance, both from the side of light and the side of darkness. Paradoxically, this is happening at a time when the last remnants of humanity's awareness of the supersensible has been extinguished. A mighty change must permeate humanity if it is to realise and master its present destiny.

Where is Christianity in this immense interplay of forces and why does it not intervene? Why is it not the spiritual rock on which the waves of doom and destruction break? Denominational and ecclesiastical Christianity are ineffective in the face of the challenges of this age because they are the product of different times. When the Catholic and Protestant churches were founded, the very modern problems we now face did not exist. There were no

8. THE WORLD SITUATION

big cities or factories. There was no mass media or modern forms of transportation that have helped to shrink the world. There was no electricity, and neither were there atomic bombs. Because of this, Christianity has yet to find the form that will help it deal with the destinies of our present age. It can only be culturally fruitful if it keeps pace with the developments of the times, and if its inner and outer forms – its spiritual content and how it is presented to the world – are also up to date.

Three obstacles prevent Christianity from intervening effectively at the present time. The first is traditionalism. This sees Christianity as only a sum of time-honoured traditions, and, indeed, what would we be as Christians if we did not look back reverently to the events in Palestine two thousand years ago? Christ's incarnation, death and resurrection, no matter how unnoticed they may have been at the time, form the historical foundation upon which all of Christian life rests. But looking back to a sacred past is no longer sufficient. The historical figure of Jesus of Nazareth, if we understand him correctly, leads us out of an inner necessity to search for Christ in the present. We must endeavour to meet him where he is today. No doubt he already has a much more powerful effect on people's lives than we realise.

But breaking free from the spell of traditionalism is not too difficult. Tradition no longer exercises the kind of power over modern humanity that it used to and has thus largely been emptied of substance. The next stage of Christianity, beyond Catholicism and Protestantism, will be a Christianity that stands on the threshold of the spiritual world as the veil that conceals it from our sight is drawn aside. Humanity today is not only faced with unprecedented new problems, but also with unprecedented new experiences. But because we do not yet have the proper concepts to take hold of them, they are ignored and soon forgotten.

The second stumbling block is dogmatism, which came about through the separation of faith and knowledge at the height of the Middle Ages. During this time humanity began to develop the intellect through the investigation of nature and its desire to master the surrounding world. However, the leading ecclesiastical thinkers insisted that religious truth, or knowledge acquired through revelation, remain a matter of faith overseen by the Church. Secular truth, or knowledge arrived at by reason, departed from the divine and became fundamentally atheistic.

Dogmatism not only afflicts the ecclesiastical view of religious truth, it also affects the intellect that was emancipated by the separation of faith and knowledge. This may have led to the emergence of natural science and technology, but it also established a thinly veiled world of lies, equipping humanity with a cleverness that can prove or disprove anything as required. For example, it runs riot in modern propaganda, which is an insult to human dignity and free thought. Today, there is still a widespread refusal to recognise that the emancipated intellect is incapable of producing constructive, healing ideas. It is suitable only for analysis and negation, and though no one wants to recognise this yet, leads more towards falsehood than to truth. Indeed, the materialistic worldview is an objective untruth because it takes what is only a partial aspect of reality and declares it to be the totality of world existence.

Both the backwardness of church dogma and modern intellectualism's dangerous one-sidedness can be attributed to traditional Christianity. The Church withdrew from its responsibility to develop thought in science and technology, retreating instead behind dogma. Humanity's entire spiritual future now depends on overcoming the separation of faith and knowledge. Thinking has become godless because it has become human-less. The smarter we became, the more intelligence became devoid of soul. Thinking became automatic, so to speak, running according to the laws of mathematics and mechanics.

If thinking is to become Christian, and thus constructive and healing, we must permeate it with our innermost being. Real spirit will then enter our thoughts again and we will be able to grasp the world's spiritual content, not merely its material exterior. Our spiritual being, awakened in thought, becomes the organ for the forgotten spiritual being of the world. Rudolf Steiner's world-historical significance lies in the fact that from his epistemological writings of the 1880s onwards, and then in the breadth of his development of a new spiritual worldview, he initiated and prepared the way for the salvation, restoration and Christianisation of human thought. The separation of faith and knowledge

8. THE WORLD SITUATION

can be overcome. The way is open for a perceiving, knowing Christianity that casts off the stumbling block of dogmatism.

The third stumbling block is the spiritual egoism that has taken hold of traditional Christian life. It was a world-historical necessity that the age of personal Christianity began with the days of Bernard of Clairvaux and even more so with those of Martin Luther. Ultimately, however, that led to a narrowing of Christian sensibilities. In broad circles, the mood developed that Christianity was primarily about the individual soul finding forgiveness and salvation from sin. The supra-personal, cosmic significance of the Mystery of Golgotha receded from people's view. Ever since the current Michael age announced itself, pointing with dramatic force from the personal to the supra-personal, many people have struggled to distinguish the true meaning of Christianity from the blissful egoism that has penetrated it. Theology itself has described the difficulty of finding the path from faith to love.

Today, however, looking back on the so-called 'century of socialism' that has passed since 1848, we must admit that amid advancing chaos, Christianity has not yet made its specific contribution to solving social questions and developing a genuine, culturally viable way of building a community. That contribution will remain lacking so long as we do not overcome the egoistic principle at the core of Christianity.

Christianity will only get away from the religious egoism that prevents it from making a specific contribution to solving social problems to the extent that it takes on a sacramental character. Sacramentalism has its meaning in the sanctification of the whole of life in all its provinces. Grasping the supra-personal sphere is inherent in Christianity. One is not just a Christian for oneself but for the world. Sacramentalism fulfils the ideal of the general priesthood of all believers. Even the Reformation groped for the sphere that would overcome the egoism of personal salvation. The gracious intervention of a higher world opens up the possibility of Christianising all human existence.

The true spirit of the age is, in essence, Christ himself. He has entered into a new closeness to humanity, bringing the whole world of the supersensible to our earthly shores. Michael, the archangel of the age, precedes him as a forerunner and herald. Because Christian life must be wrested from the demons that have been unleashed in our time, Michael wants to give it a martial character. Instead of weakness and fear, he wants to grant souls courage. Where we overcome traditionalism, Michael tears open the heavens and we experience the Risen One as newly present. An apocalyptic era begins. Michael shows himself as the prince of free human thought when we overcome dogmatism through a living, knowing Christianity. By overcoming soul egoism with sacramental Christianity, it will be possible to wrest the future of humanity from the opposing powers. Instead of Bolshevism and capitalism, Christianity must shape the future of humanity. Where that begins, Christ walks through the world healing, as he did two thousand years ago in human form. He does so today in spiritual form, laying his hands on the wounds from which humanity is bleeding.

9
The Millennium
(1950)

As the twentieth century approached, a mood of anticipation moved through people's souls. There had been rapid developments in industry, technology, transport and trade, and many people felt as if they were being swept along on a wave of almost supra-personal force rather than simply advancing through their own ingenuity and inventiveness alone. But there was more to their anticipation than just their hope and optimism about progress. People expected something far-reaching to take place. Perhaps if a naïvely complacent materialism had not dulled people's senses and made their thoughts earth-bound, then more of them might have felt that they were teetering on the brink of revelation. Mixed with the anticipation of what was to come was a desire to take stock of the century that was coming to an end.

In 1900, there were many works that looked back over the last one hundred years. Was it not a strange path that the preceding century seemed to have taken from the light and Olympian splendour of Goethe and German idealism to the more prosaic sobriety of the advancing scientific-technical age? Had we left behind a paradise or just an otherworldly, dreamlike illusion? This experience was also associated with a new alertness and a feeling of individual freedom: hardly anyone sensed a farewell or mourned the past.

It is difficult to say if people at the time associated the anticipated greatness of the new period with it being the final century before the turn of the millennium. Perhaps that thought only comes to mind now given that we have experienced the major shifts that have occurred since then, and we can more clearly see how the significant changes that the new century would bring were foreshadowed in an unspecified way. Here at the midpoint, we also have a sense of further changes approaching.

Because working with decimal systems is a relatively recent innovation, we might think that the division of history into centuries and millennia is more of a modern abstract construction, one that corresponds less to the actual rhythms of development than did those ideas of older times. Those times summarised groups of years according to other principles of division, above all according to a system based on the number seven. However, the rhythm of a hundred years, and especially a thousand, must also be based on objective lawfulness, on a spiritual archetype. It cannot be unimportant, for example, that the metaphor of the millennium, the period of a thousand years, occurs in the Revelation to John. This rhythm is reflected in external earthly events, and when we survey the great course of human history, the times at which the millennia are fulfilled stand out to us as clear turning points and periods of transition.

But we also notice how fear and anxiety are particularly heightened in people's souls at these junctures. End-time moods sweep through them and cause them to pile up notable earthly achievements as if they wanted to build a dam against a destructive deluge they feel is approaching. The 'end of the world' has repeatedly happened when old soul forces, still emerging from the superhuman cosmic realm, ebbed away and states of consciousness faded. It is difficult for souls to part with the old powers because they perceive them as great. Yet only by relinquishing them can a further step be taken in the development of personality and ego. The desire to hold on to the old manifests outwardly as a drive for greatness and the accumulation of earthly power and splendour.

As the third pre-Christian millennium dawned, an irrepressible building impulse emerged in the people of the Near East that found expression in the Babylonian ziggurats and the Egyptian pyramids. In the Bible we read about the Tower of Babylon. In their semi-mythical descriptions, the books of the Old Testament also reveal the psychological motivations that led to these towering structures: a struggle against the divine will and a convulsive desire to hold onto a world doomed to destruction. Behind earthly greatness is fear, and this greatness expresses itself as megalomania.

At that turn of that millennium, the doomsday mood also

9. THE MILLENNIUM

asserted itself. Antiquity's numerous legends and traditions about the Great Flood refer to this time in the same way as the tower-building myth. American and German excavations in Ur and Uruk have uncovered a fossilised layer of mud that has established there were indeed floods of gigantic proportions in the Euphrates–Tigris region at that time. However, according to Rudolf Steiner's descriptions, an inner soul experience of being inundated also occurred and was widespread among people. The old clairvoyance that had sustained humanity until then suddenly died out. According to the traditions and prophecies of the East, the Kali Yuga, or Dark Age, began at that time (Steiner gives the year 3101 BC). The new intellectual consciousness could not unfold its light as quickly as the old dream-related vision was being extinguished. Intensified by great natural disasters, people were overcome by an inner darkness and a feeling of powerlessness in which they thought they were drowning.

The next millennium does not stand out with the same elemental force. It is the time of Abraham. In the figure of the biblical patriarch, a significant branch of humanity, conscious of its future task, broke away from the ancient magical world of Mesopotamia and Egypt because these civilisations were now doomed. In the inconspicuous land of Jordan, the foundations were laid for a future civilisation that reckoned with the human intellect. The titanic building impulses of the previous millennium were abandoned. In the patriarchal period, a simple 'hut culture' emerged as the basis of a great turning inwards for human beings, while close by, in Sodom and Gomorrah, sulphurous fires destroyed a world wallowing in ancient opulence.

King David and the Greek poet Homer stood at the beginning of the previous pre-Christian millennium. Each of them represents a stream that contributed to the downfall of a world that had grown old and was past its time. In the eastern Mediterranean, the turn of the millennium was preceded by large migrations of peoples, which seem like the labour pains that accompanied the birth of Europe from the womb of Mother Asia. In the burning of Troy, Homer describes the downfall of an entire ancient stage of humanity, which was then replaced by the thoughtful and beauty-loving Greeks. King David replaced the atavistic ecstasy of the Philistines and Canaanites with the intellectual and moral element of the Israelite-Jewish stream. Solomon's temple was built following a wave of Phoenician building impulses through which the humanity of the Near East wanted to entrench and defend itself against its downfall. At the same time, the temple was also a prophetic architectural symbol for the newly rising future. As the dwelling place of the deity, it pointed to the future human body in which the eagerly awaited Messiah would appear among other human beings.

A thousand years later came the great turning point of time. As it approached, the feeling of the end of the world emerged in the form of an intense religious longing for redemption. That feeling was the dark undercurrent of Messianic expectation. It ran through the nations in various guises, sometimes in quiet piety, but mostly in fear-driven impatience. The rise of the Diadochi tyrants of Syria, later successors of Alexander the Great against whom the freedom fighters of the Maccabean period defended themselves, and the Roman Caesars who shed the first Christian martyrs' blood, all resulted from a Messianic feeling that had crossed over into the political arena. They became diabolical counterimages of the true Messiah. Once again, an insatiable construction frenzy, driven by Caesar's madness, revealed the death throes of an old world struggling against its end.

Towards the end of the first Christian millennium, a great fear of the end of the world remained. Even within a humanity in which the power of Christ was working, a new stage of human consciousness still had to wrestle its way to the surface. The urge to persist in the old ways had hardened souls like a thick crust and it took a long time before this new stage could break through. The Huns, Arabs and Mongols who burst into Europe were like weather signs before and after the actual storm of rebirth in souls. In the Crusades, in the founding of the new monastic movements and the reform and mendicant orders, there was a flicker of the new that aimed at a flaming spirituality. The vast, dusky forests gave way to the wide, bright expanses of meadows and fields around the towns that were suddenly springing up everywhere. But fear of the times, whipped up by plague epidemics, also manifested itself in the wild processions of flagellants, howling through city streets as they scourged themselves bloody.

The transition in which we currently find ourselves, the final

9. THE MILLENNIUM

century of the second Christian millennium, has its own characteristics. We must go back five millennia in history to arrive at an upheaval of corresponding intensity and significance. (We will leave out the great turning point of time at the beginning of the Christian era because it belongs to a different order of magnitude.) The same ancient traditions and prophecies that predicted the beginning of the Kali Yuga at the start of the third millennium BC also spoke of an 'Age of Light' that would replace it after five thousand years, at the beginning of our twentieth century. According to this great primordial calendar, which today's spiritual research confirms as accurate, the year before the transition from the nineteenth to the twentieth century was a much more significant turning point in the development of humanity than people at the time were able to grasp. In 1899, the five thousand years of the Kali Yuga, which began in 3101 BC, came to an end. Only in vague premonitions did the dawning of a new age flash through people's souls. Given that transition, we can say that humanity had a century to prepare itself for the decisions that the next millennium would bring with the first breakthroughs and achievements of the new, brighter age. Those who consider only the external course of history will find it paradoxical, even nonsensical, to assert that we have entered a brighter age. It is only when we penetrate behind the scenes of outer events to consider the evolution of human consciousness that we find a key to the secrets of the present.

Five thousand years ago, at the time of the Egyptian-Babylonian 'tower building' and the 'Great Flood', the ancient clairvoyance disappeared. With the sensory and intellectual consciousness that was then beginning to develop, humanity grew into a great 'confusion of languages', as described in the Old Testament myth. However, only in that way could the path to individual freedom be found. In the meantime, the twilight of the gods descended ever more deeply as the world of the supersensible increasingly eluded human consciousness. The triumphant advance of modern science and technology signalled a final step in human consciousness becoming completely earthbound. The seemingly unshakeable edifice of materialistic civilisation that greeted the dawning of the twentieth century was the final achievement of the Kali Yuga. Then the earthquakes and storms of destiny set in, leaving its seemingly fortress-like structure a desolate field of rubble. All the suffering and destruction of our time reveal their meaning – and God's underlying purpose – if we see in them the birth pangs of a new consciousness. During the millennia of the Dark Age, humanity developed the free, individual personality; now it must regain perception and awareness of the supersensible world. The materialistic worldview must be replaced by one that encompasses both the sensory and supersensible worlds. Such a worldview would also help us understand the material side of creation more deeply through a consideration of its spiritual context. The ability of souls to direct their thoughts and, ultimately, their perceptive faculties towards the supersensible world will itself be the source from which the new Age of Light will arise amid the thunder and lightning storms of the present time

The tension and contrast between the outer course of events and the inner meaning of this new Age of Light are greater today than at any other time in world history. Each millennium of the Dark Age marked a further descent of human consciousness. The turn of the millennium to the year 2000 will be the first that should bring about a step in the resurgence of human consciousness. How can we harmonise such a hopeful outlook with our current fateful circumstances?

Thus far, the events of the twentieth century have been frightening, and can easily arouse in us a fear of the future, just as such a fear was associated with the doomsday moods of earlier millennia. Since 1900, changes and upheavals of such a radical nature have taken place at the level of the life of nations alone that all expressions that can be coined for them remain entirely inadequate. Although the old orders and borders had already begun to dissolve before the First World War, the process was accelerated by its outbreak and the aftermath. Despite the emergence of the social questions posed by industrialisation, political and social living conditions remained largely as they had been during the previous centuries. But when the first tremors of the great earthquake set in, it became clear that all orders were only apparent. The edifice of modern civilisation was undermined and quickly collapsed.

9. THE MILLENNIUM

Today, chaos has taken hold of the entire world and shaken the lives of nations. In Europe and the colonial empires administered by European countries, all previous state orders and economic property and power relations have crumbled. The end of the British Empire is only the most striking example. Even the empires of the Asian continent, such as China and India, based on ancient sacred traditions, resemble fields through which the plough of fate has mercilessly passed without leaving any evident furrows for the sowing of the future.

Clearly, the chaos in people's lives is is a consequence of these processes not a cause of them. If one only looks at some partial phenomena, one can still think these are the consequences of political high-handedness or omissions. To look at the chaos in its entirety, we must look for the causes on a higher plane. We begin to understand that the store of ideas that gave rise to the previous arrangements was used up, and the old ideas no longer had an organising effect. A vacuum arose into which all the old systems fell.

Those who have the power to survey the overall chaos feel compelled to look for the spiritual sphere, from which we can draw new ideas. This necessity can flare up in our souls, especially when we see the dangerous polarity and tension emerging within the stormy waves of the overall chaos with which East and West face each other today. They collide in Europe, where this polarity should find a centre and a balance. To think that we can solve the East–West problem in the external fields of political and economic life would be one of the most disastrously superficial and thoughtless things to do. It is clear that only a spiritual solution can move us forward. The struggle between two different spiritualities – or un-spiritualities – manifests itself in both latent and open tensions.

The total change in world conditions that the twentieth century has already brought about, however, reaches far beyond the level of the life of nations. Today it no longer sounds fantastic to point out that even the climate and the regular rhythmic sequence of the seasons have been drawn into the great upheaval. Cosmic disturbances seem to be at work, and the earth is no longer the all-forgiving, all-loving mother. Is the collapse of the human order now affecting the natural order, or are the cosmic disturbances that are making themselves felt in meteorological upheavals causing chaos among people?

Even the force field of earth's rhythmic life cannot be regarded today as the actual level of causes. Like the chaotic life of the nations, it is only a level of consequences. We only rise to the level of causes when we look at the changes that have occurred in the supersensible environment of human and natural life since the beginning of the century.

Our materialistic way of thinking still holds us captive so that we are not prepared to reckon with the reality of a supersensible world without a violent jolt of awakening. This is true even for those people who do confess a religious faith. They do not question the fact that the miracles in which they believe remain entirely incomprehensible for the simple reason that people like to believe in miracles. Yet neither in science nor in the church are people led to a consistent rethinking of their worldview.

In our time, millions of souls have had to leave the earthly world abruptly. The world of the deceased forms an immeasurably dense cloud over our heads. Compared to the quiet time before 1900 that fact alone must have fundamentally changed the supersensible environment and filled it with tension and drama. Humanity on earth today has reached a null point in its feeling for and understanding of the world of the deceased, just when that world has experienced an intensification not seen for many millennia.

The gigantic vortices that agitate the supersensible sphere of humanity include those forces unleashed by the triumphant advances of technology during our century. Humanity has learnt to work admirably with electricity, which was virtually unknown before the twentieth century. Based on the concepts of natural science to date, it is impossible to know what electricity actually is. At best, we can only grope for the essence of this force with hypothetical constructions.

In reality, the essence of electricity no longer belongs to the realm of the sensory world. It is of a non-sensory – or more precisely, a sub-sensory – nature and can only be truly grasped through a view of the world that has escaped the spell of mere sense perception and encompasses the world of the super- and non-sensory.

9. THE MILLENNIUM

Even more so, atomic energy, the most far-reaching discovery of our century, cannot be understood in its essence and, therefore, cannot really be mastered without knowing what lies beyond the realm of the senses. Without fully realising it, modern physics and technology have unleashed cosmic forces that had previously remained latent and poured them into the supersensible atmosphere in which we live. It does not take much imagination to recognise that generating atomic energy already sets in motion processes that affect people and the earth, even if they do not take the form of nuclear bombs.

We children of the twentieth century live in a supersensible atmosphere that has been changed through and through. The supersensible ocean in which we are immersed has begun to surge violently around us. It is no wonder that today, as at the turn of the previous millennia, megalomania flares up here and there. The demons of a perishing world are rebelling against this stormily advancing destiny.

If we remain mesmerised by individual strokes of fate and catastrophes of the times, from which we may also have to suffer personally, we will not be able to make sense of the talk of the dawning of an Age of Light. People will think that the world has never been as dark and full of distress as it is now. But perhaps we can get a sense of the sunrise that lies hidden behind the stormy skies if we take in the scale and scope of the upheavals shaking the world today. If one does this, one can receive a glimpse of the new light that shines into the world from supersensible spheres.

The sunrise that ushers in the new Age of Light, no matter how tragically veiled it may be, is not brought about by some impersonal cosmic potency. This sunrise is the most personal deity, the incarnation of Divine Love itself. The spheres of the supersensible are in a state of surging motion, beating against the shores of the physical world like a stormy sea. The reason is that a mighty divine being is entering a new proximity to the human world. What has been described and expected by the gospels and the Revelation to John as the Second Coming of Christ is to be fulfilled in our time in the supersensible. The darker and more sinister layers of the approaching supersensible world reach and test us today such that the lighter powers and beings of the supersensible world, particularly the sun-like Christ being itself, are hidden behind them. Yet that is nothing other than what the old traditions expressed when they said that the revelation of the Antichrist must precede the return of Christ.

From our time onwards, Christ wants to bring about an enormous upward turn for earthly human consciousness, just as he brought about the turnaround for the continuing development of humanity's being through his physical incarnation two thousand years ago. The first two thousand years of Christian development still belonged to the Kali Yuga, the Age of Darkness. The meaning of the twentieth century is that the approaching sun of a new revelation of Christ will bring about the dawning of a new Age of Light, albeit amid great storms and earthquakes.

All the chaos and catastrophic collapses of the present are the consequences of the decline in consciousness during the Age of Darkness. The traditional Christian streams are partly to blame for the tragic situation in which we find ourselves. By separating knowledge received through faith and revelation from knowledge received through reason and the senses, they narrowed the horizon of human consciousness, confining it to the earthly realm, where it succumbed to the materialistic worldview, instead of expanding and strengthening it for the ascent into the spiritual world.

The intention of Christ's new revelation, which is the real meaning of our age, is to redeem not only our lives but, first and foremost, our consciousness. The first step in the redemption and Christianisation of human consciousness will be to look to the supersensible world because that is not only where we will find the causes of chaos that surrounds us, but also the scene of Christ's new revelation. The sphere of Christ's latest revelation will also become the source of creative ideas for the rest of the century and the future millennium. From it, we can slowly plant new systems in the debris fields of earthly life.

10

The Age of Light
(1953)

Where do we stand today in the serious dramas of our time? A sublime prelude began in 1879 when the age of Gabriel was replaced by the age of Michael, when the archangel of the moon handed over guidance of humanity to the archangel of the sun. The Michael age was inaugurated with the archangel's victory in the spiritual sphere closest to our earthly existence. The Ahrimanic dragon forces were defeated and cast down into the depths, which cleared the way for the archangel to enter earthly humanity. Michael had long awaited this moment. He wanted to follow Christ, who had united himself with the earth through his resurrection and ascension, and be his herald on earth. Through this heraldic service, the effects of Christ's working would be raised into human consciousness.

But the Ahrimanic powers were also on earth following their defeat by Michael and thus began the spiritual battle that is characteristic of our age: the war between the sons of light and the sons of darkness.

At first, darkness still covered the earth from primaeval times. According to the ancient traditions this was the Kali Yuga, the Age of Darkness. As the new century approached, the veil of darkness lifted and light flooded in. Thus, the transition to the twentieth century brought about a complete collaboration between Christ and Michael. Just as John the Baptist once went before Christ to prepare the way for him on earth, so does Michael go before him today as the herald of Christ in the etheric realm. From indications given by Rudolf Steiner, numerous people, including those who founded The Christian Community, knew that a significant stage in Christ's approach to humanity would fall in 1933. Humanity experienced the terrible shadow of that event, unable to see the great light by which it was cast. The darkness that Michael overcame in the spiritual world in the nineteenth century must now be penetrated on earth by people themselves. The battle is now raging between the Ahrimanic inventions of modern civilisation and the Michaelic intuitions, the new spirit-thoughts, which at first can only show themselves in embryonic form.

Beginning in our century, young people have come to the forefront of Christian history. In their prenatal existence they witnessed how the etheric sphere brightened with the rising of the spiritual sun. Imbued with this sunlight, they were born on earth and entered a culture woven from darkness. This gave rise to the youth movement's various stages. The young people stood opposed to this culture, although at first only with a dull will. They still lacked the light of a clear and articulate thinking. The forces of darkness had seized people's thoughts, and only those thoughts directed towards the sense-perceptible were available. In the youth movement, therefore, goodwill lived without concepts.

But then something new emerged. Humanity had already received the first great gift from Michael: the inspiration that led to anthroposophy. This gave young people the concepts they needed, and the first beginnings of a marriage of goodwill with the new Michaelic thoughts came about.

By the end of the twentieth century the cold flood of Ahrimanic thoughts along with their impact on modern technology will reach a climax. At the same time, the power of new thoughts arising out of the illumination of the spiritual realm must increase. When three times 666 years have passed since the beginning of Christianity, the fate of humanity must be decided for the future.

Now, after the middle of the twentieth century, what a blessing awaits us! Michael is here! Christ is here! Michael wants to kindle the light of thought in our souls, through which souls will see not only the spiritual in all earthly existence, but Christ himself. Michael's concern is that human thinking should cease to be merely intellectual; it should be permeated by the will and be thought by the whole human being. Rudolf Steiner expresses this as follows:

> Michael liberates thought from the sphere of the head; he clears the way for it to the heart ... The Age of Michael has dawned. Hearts are beginning to have thoughts; spiritual fervour is now proceeding, not merely from

10. THE AGE OF LIGHT

mystical obscurity, but from souls clarified by thought. To understand this means to receive Michael into the heart. Thoughts which at the present time strive to grasp the Spiritual must originate in hearts which beat for Michael as the fiery Prince of Thought in the Universe.[1]

A different way of thinking is being born. It does not give answers right away; it remains in a questioning mood so that answers arise only with the right questions.

People today bring the germ of Michaelic thoughts into their earthly existence. When we reflect on our past at specific points in our lives, or make decisions for the future, we may observe how our will rises from the depths of our soul and our thoughts come to meet it. When the two unite, Michael's gaze meets us. It is he who teaches our hearts to think. In such gazes, from our present time onwards, people will see the sphere in which Michael and Christ are to be found. Michael gives the light; Christ provides the warmth. Michael conveys the seriousness of inner resolve; Christ confers the grace that our soul receives. Michael speaks to our courage; we approach Christ in humility.

Just as a child has their guardian angel, so young people will have a bright double beside them: the Archangel Michael. The Old Testament story of Tobias accompanied by the Archangel Raphael is a kind of prophecy for us. The person of today can say, 'I was born into a time in which I meet Christ and Michael as contemporaries, as fellow inhabitants of the earth. I must pay attention to those moments when perhaps only a very thin veil separates me from them, and if I cultivate an inner trust the veil will part and I will see them walking beside me.' In this we see an image of earlier times when people knew they had the gods as guests at their tables. Through this new closeness to the heavens the world is rejuvenated.

> Walk while you have the light, before darkness overtakes you. Whoever walks in the dark does not know where they are going. Believe in the light while you have the light, so that you may become children of light.
> (John 12:35f)

11
Michael and the New Coming of Christ
(1953)

Christ's death and resurrection initiated an evolutionary ascent not only for human beings but for all earthly existence. But that does not mean it reversed our fall into original sin in one go. Only that which is Christianised within each individual person can be snatched from the abyss. This battle has raged since Christ's Easter victory, and the more the circle of light grows, the more powerfully the forces of darkness appear on the scene. The history of humanity and the earth since the event of Golgotha is determined by the increasing tension between Christ's *parousia*, his Second Coming, and the coming of the Antichrist, the *apostasia*, as described in Paul's Second Letter to the Thessalonians. This battle will continue until the end of the earthly aeon. Then, the 'separation of the spirits' will culminate in a cosmic event of the greatest magnitude.

The 'new earth', the part of the earth's existence that is connected to Christ and transformed by him, will emerge from the world conflagration like a phoenix. By tearing itself away from the heaviness and power of death, it will create the new, shining, sun-like form of our planet. What is left untransformed will be discarded, like a cinder of the moon, and remain subject to the law of gravity and death.

Paul speaks of this in Chapter 15 in his First Letter to the Corinthians, the great resurrection chapter. The power that germinates incorruptible life and a new spiritual corporeality entered earthly evolution at Easter and now flows through all future development. Just as a mortal race descended from the first Adam, which increasingly fell under the spell of death, so the second Adam becomes the ancestor of a resurrected race which, through the power of the spirit over matter, brings to growth the germ of a new, indestructible life. Then, finally, the time will come when Christ's Easter victory over death will be repeated on

11. MICHAEL AND THE NEW COMING OF CHRIST

human, earthly, and cosmic levels. As the last enemy, death will be overcome (1Cor. 15:26).

On the path that leads from Golgotha to the end of earth evolution, there will be a stage in which the outcome of the final decision will be prefigured. The age in which this will take place will have an apocalyptic character, marked to a special degree by the *parousia*, the so-called Second Coming of Christ.

Paul must have felt more at home in that future age – our present one – than in his own time. As one born out of due time (1Cor. 15:8), Paul was more a contemporary of the age of the consciousness soul. As a result, he became the herald of Christ's *parousia*.

At the climax of the great battle the mystery of the 'Day of the Lord' will be revealed, but it will not be an outwardly perceptible day that one will be able to date. Rather, there will be a 'day' in the supersensible realm of the etheric, the realm of formative life forces. Human souls will be blind to it at first, then the darkness that has held sway will come to an end. Daybreak is coming, heralded by a dawn. This will be around the time indicated by the ancient Asian prophecies that speak of the transition from a five-thousand-year Age of Darkness, the Kali Yuga, to an Age of Light.

During this time the opposing powers will reach a high point, utilising humanity's cold cunning to make the dark wall of the material world, with its fascinating riches and technological possibilities, denser and more impenetrable. At first, the Antichrist has the advantage. Although he and his hosts are not of 'flesh and blood' (Eph. 6:12) but of a supersensible nature, he performs his magic arts in the sensory realm, casting a spell of deception and delusion over people. Christ's evolution and working, however, are entirely hidden in the etheric realm, meaning people can pass them by unaware. Fascinated by what brings them disaster after disaster, ruin after ruin, people are in danger of sleeping through what is occurring in the spiritual realm for the sake of their salvation.

The ancient prophecies already point to this, saying that the Antichrist's coming precedes the coming of Christ. Paul builds on this. Christ is already present in the etheric, but the adversary attempts to forestall awareness of him among incarnated human beings. He does everything he can to distract souls from the sphere in which the decisive miracle of the spiritual sun takes place. Paul touches on the deepest mysteries of destiny when he says that it corresponds to the will of Providence itself when humanity passes through a time in which the tendencies of deception reach the peak of their power: 'God sends them the fully unfolded power of deception', or as the Luther Bible drastically puts it, 'God will send them strong delusions so that they will believe the lie' (2Thess. 2:11). Deception's magic causes people, both in their striving for knowledge and in their cultural and civilisational practice, to regard only the material aspect of the world and human beings as the truth. They deny the sphere of the supersensible world that is the scene of Christ's *parousia*.

The Antichrist, the satanic-Ahrimanic power of the lie that claims to be truth, does not itself enter the sense-perceptible realm, but where it gains influence over human souls, it finds expression in a particular type of person. Paul calls this the 'man of chaos' (*ánthropos tēs anomías*), and through such a person, the 'magic of chaos' (*mystērion tēs anomías*) works. Its ultimate creator is the 'spirit of chaos', 'chaos personified' (*ho ánomos*) according to Paul (2 Thess. 2:3, 7 and 8).

Here, the Luther Bible is far removed from the conciseness of Paul. Starting from the Latin text, it translates the concept of *anomía* as 'sin' and 'malice', as in 'the man of sin', 'the mystery of wickedness', and 'the malicious one'. However, we are by no means talking about the 'moral evil' these expressions denote. We are talking about 'objective evil'. This objective evil acts as the power of the 'intellectual fall' into sin when thinking follows only the laws of cold cleverness, of soulless spirit.[1] Has not this one-sidedness penetrated the development of science to a very great extent over the last few centuries? And from the field of thought, objective evil has taken hold of all areas of modern civilisation and become 'social evil'.

The Greek word *anomías* literally means 'lawlessness'. How this word resounds in the mouth of Paul! Paul is up in arms against the tyranny of the Mosaic law because it keeps people immature and unfree; he well knows the spirit of freedom that comes from the 'inner lawgiver', the 'Christ in us'. But even more so than the law of Moses, Paul fights against the power that aims to dissolve *all* lawfulness. Indeed, he fights against the

11. MICHAEL AND THE NEW COMING OF CHRIST

external law and its letter because he foresees how it prepares the way for the spirit of chaos and the dissolution of all laws.

In our time, what Paul means is almost palpable. Today, external law flows into modern political and social legislation and into the scientific evaluation of nature's laws. Daily we see more clearly an unstoppable process of dissolution and chaos in all areas of the law, in all previous orders and harmonies. People want to organise modern life by constantly introducing new laws. But due to the unmanageable abundance of laws we lose the law's binding force, and in places where we believe that we have achieved notable triumphs in the research and technical application of the laws at work in material existence, we are already working with destructive forces that no one truly understands.

The ecclesiastical streams have long been on the defensive and do not realise that their attempts to preserve the old will be hopeless in the long run. They leave perceptive thinking and civilisation's development to the outside world. Thus, instead of fighting with the Ahrimanic power in the arena of thinking and as it appears in the scientific worldview, they allow the achievements of anti-Christian intelligence into their realm.

Paul speaks prophetically of the Christ events unfolding behind the curtain of the sensory world. In some places, his apocalyptic imagery seems to be describing a single, fixed moment in the future upon which these decisive events will converge. Paul himself, when he was immersed in the eschatology of the Pharisees, had the idea that the Last Day would arrive, lightning-like, as a tremendous outer catastrophe: graves would open and the dead would rise to final judgement.

Perhaps the words he uses here are similar in some respects to those that were customary in the Pharisees' circle. But now he pulls back the curtain to reveal processes unfolding in the spiritual world, processes that we are in the middle of today. They are full of dramatic tension, moving inexorably towards their decisive culmination, and just as it was for Paul in the noon-day hour of Damascus, so will these processes also find their fulfilment in a flash: for a few individuals at first, then later for all of humanity. But rather than being the work of a single moment, they will continue to unfold until the end of the world.

The misunderstanding of such a world event arises for those who take what Paul says in a literal, and therefore purely external, way: 'Listen, I tell you a mystery: we will not all sleep, but we will all be changed'. Here, the Luther Bible continues: 'and suddenly, in a moment, at the time of the last trumpet' (1Cor. 15:51f).

What is meant is the unheard-of transformation through which the person united with Christ acquires a share in Christ's resurrection body. The mystery of the 'spiritual human being' comes over individuals in a powerful way, whether they are in their earthly bodies or in the realm of the dead. Then, the power of Christ's presence takes hold of them so that they are lifted beyond space and time.

The two Greek words that Luther translates as 'suddenly' and 'in a moment' are not temporal terms. The first, *en atómo* ('in the atom', 'indivisible'), is a spatial concept; it denotes space shrunk down to a final, indivisible dimension. Similarly, the word 'moment' is the final smallest measure of a temporal sequence. In stepping out of space and time, the human being is seized by the transformative power of Christ's perpetual presence.

The words 'at the time of the last trumpet' refer to a particular phase of future development. Paul uses the same imagery that characterises John's apocalyptic language, but it is precisely in looking at the last book of the Bible that we can see that the sounding of the seventh trumpet in no way signifies the 'Last Day' as a decisive endpoint.

Firstly, the sounding of the seventh trumpet accompanies the unfolding apocalyptic drama of an entire world age. Secondly, the seventh trumpet is followed by the pouring out of the golden bowls of wrath from the heavenly temple throughout seven periods. As in the Apocalypse, when Paul mentions the seventh trumpet, he refers to a specific future time. It is precisely the time that Paul, through his nature, was already living in in advance: our present age of the consciousness soul, when the battle with the Antichrist reaches its culmination. Paul's First Letter to the Thessalonians contains an apocalyptic reference similar to his First Letter to the Corinthians, which takes us further: 'For the Lord himself will come down from heaven, with a loud command, with the voice of the archangel and with the trumpet call of God' (1Thess. 4:16).

11. MICHAEL AND THE NEW COMING OF CHRIST

Here, Paul is talking about Michael. The figure of this archangel also appears in John's Apocalypse when the seventh trumpet sounds and the battle reaches its culmination. Michael fights against the dragon for Christ, the spiritual sun, and achieves victory in heaven. On earth, the overthrown adversary splits into the double beast that rises from the sea and the land. The people associated with Christ continue Michael's heavenly battle on earth, in particular the fight against the deceptions of the satanic-Ahrimanic power, the 'objective evil'.

So, if we want to relate the apocalyptic references of Paul's letters to a specific historical epoch, we arrive at the Michael age. It began in the last third of the nineteenth century within the age of the consciousness soul. These are the centuries in which we live and whose culminating time of decision we are approaching. In his apocalyptic *Fairy Tale of the Green Snake and the Beautiful Lily*, Goethe has already proclaimed that our time awaits a 'command'. When the words 'The time has come' ring out for the third time, then the great sacrifice is due, and the transformation begins.

Paul himself never tired of addressing this call to awake and to take up arms to human souls. He sounds it most succinctly, like a trumpet blast himself, in his Letter to the Ephesians by taking up an old mystery summons:

> Wake up, sleeper,
> rise from the dead,
> and Christ will shine on you.
> (Eph. 5:14)

In ancient times, in the temples of initiation, the hierophant raised the neophyte from the three-day temple sleep with these words. The newly initiated rose from the grave, transformed in consciousness and their very being. Yet what a turnaround has now occurred in humanity's inner history! The disciple no longer finds enlightenment isolated from life, unfree and subject to the authoritative, hypnotic guidance of their soul. As their own hierophant, the seeker must find the path to Christ in the midst of life without disturbing their ordinary consciousness. The wake-up call should not awaken them from the somnambulistic sleep of the temple, but from the sleep of the senses, which we think is wakefulness. We must awaken to a higher consciousness without giving up our daytime consciousness, which is a kind of sleep as far as the spiritual world is concerned. It is a mistake and a fatal laziness, even cowardice towards the supersensible world, if the Pauline apocalyptic wake-up calls have only ever been understood as an emotional appeal to goodwill. This talk of waking up is not merely symbolic. Paul, whom the light of Damascus enlightened, struggled with all his strength to awaken in those who listened to him the willingness and impulse for a planned training and elevation of their perceptive and discerning consciousness. He wanted to guide humanity from mere sensory perception and intellectual cognition to supersensible perception and recognition of the spirit. He wanted the spiritual human being that exists within the earthly human being to open its eyes and awaken.

Following this call to awake, Paul then calls on those to whom he is speaking to put on spiritual armour for the Michaelic battle. It is not a battle against flesh and blood but against demonic elemental forces and powers of darkness. Thus, the 'girdle of truth', the 'shield of faith', and the 'helmet of salvation' mean more than a sum of good and pious intentions. Through the most inner activity and the most faithful transformative work on our will, feelings, and thoughts, we can and should contribute to the spirit of Christ working in our true selves. He covers us as if with armour and a higher, invulnerable body consisting of our own nascent higher members. What is particularly important here is the word that the Lutheran Bible translates with the 'breastplate of righteousness'. The true, spiritual powers of life, torn from death, make us invulnerable beyond death. Spiritual science calls these forces the life spirit, which allows the lost divine archetype to shine again. It encompasses a higher being and consists of light. It is, therefore, the bearer of an illuminated consciousness. Through it, we are incorporated consciously and fully into that etheric sphere that is woven from a higher light and life, and in which the coming of Christ takes place.

12
Christians and the Conscience of the Times
(1955)

If understood correctly, conscience is the key to a profound world mystery. It comes from the Latin *conscientia*, meaning 'to know together'. It is a knowing, therefore, that a person does not do alone, but their fellow knower, the one who knows with them, is invisible. Conscience describes a person's feeling when they say to themselves, 'God sees me.'

Through our conscience, God's consciousness arises in human consciousness. That is the case not only for individuals but also for entire ages. Each age believes it knows itself, though usually it does not know itself at all. Some great individuals, such as Moses and John the Baptist, could hear the voice of the conscience of their times on behalf of humanity. The person who looks at the age together with the higher knower is aware of what is happening in it, they know what its goals and tasks are. Significant figures of the past are the interpreters and messengers of the conscience of their times.

But how can there be a conscience where there is no longer any knowledge of the one who knows with us, where humanity lives in a worldview that denies the very existence of the sphere of such a one?

If a person denies the supersensible worlds, then their innermost consciousness loses its partner; they lose the authority and standard for their entire life and striving. It is tragic when the age loses its connection with the conscience of the times through the loss of an awareness of a higher world. The lack of 'co-knowing' is born in human coexistence from the lack of knowing what lies above us. Neither in an individual's life nor in the life of the age should we be surprised that the voice of conscience falls silent when we no longer know anything about the world with which we once co-existed.

Humanity has forgotten God. It once knew him but has since forgotten the sphere in which the inspiring spirit of the age speaks specifically as the herald of that age's conscience. Thus, humanity has become unfaithful to the Godhead, not out of malice but out of forgetfulness of the supersensible world. Now, their higher co-knower, their angel, looks at the individual human being, and the archangel, as a contemporary inspiring spirit, looks at the age, and people do not realise it. A longing arises in God that people will once again notice that he is looking at them. It is like when someone gazes at another person for whom they feel interest or affection, hoping that the other person will turn around to meet their gaze. We humans disappoint the world about us. We do not turn around; our eyes do not meet. Instead of looking upwards, people today only look downwards at earthly stuff. The awareness of God, which in the times of a living conscience shone into human consciousness, is replaced by mere material awareness.

The ability to forget can, in some cases, be beneficial. For example, someone can forget their anger towards another person, or, after certain exams, they can rejoice and let go and forget everything they have learnt. However, people cannot forget their higher co-knowers, God and their angel, without tragic changes resulting in their innermost being.

We are told that what we forget sinks into our subconscious, and one has a clear feeling today that the various complexes we have forgotten are by no means benign and innocuous. Modern psychoanalysis shows how they act as causes of illness, and it is believed that these illnesses can be cured by bringing the forgotten and suppressed material back to consciousness through therapeutic conversation – the so-called 'talking cure'. Strikingly, the Swiss psychologist C. G. Jung points to the original religious character of the complexes rumbling in the human subconscious. In his theory of archetypes, he points out that the basic imagistic elements of the forgotten world of the gods are present at the bottom of human souls and, if they remain uncultivated, cause harm.

Something is being touched upon here that it would be highly

12. CHRISTIANS AND THE CONSCIENCE OF THE TIMES

worthwhile to describe in connection with a worldview that includes the supersensible.

The world of bright, pure, creative and healthy archetypes reigns over us in spirit heights. If this world is forgotten, it all too easily becomes a dark, pathogenic counterimage in the subconscious depths. The forgotten supersensible world becomes the cause of illness in the individual and the cause of dramatic apocalyptic catastrophes in the entire age. If the supersensible ocean surges and foams over the shores of the sensory world at a time when people have no organs to perceive it, then instead of experiencing the archetypal images' grace, demonic counterimages arise. A monumental simultaneity occurs: the Son of Man appears above the storm clouds, while at the same time, the beast rises from the abyss below.

Human beings must decide. If they want to find and grasp their true image, they must look for it behind the clouds of heaven, where the veil dividing the sense and supersensible worlds wants to open. We cannot be human without a view into heaven. If we lose that view, then the beast rises up and what is subhuman threatens to take possession of us all.

If people have a clear view of the Son of Man in the clouds of heaven, they can command the powers of the abyss. If they do not, they will become subservient to those powers, slaves to their own creations and institutions. The slumbering conscience of the times causes people to fall prey to the illusions and seductions rising from the depths.

We live in an age when the conscience of the times takes on a very special form. The Archangel Michael, the inspiring spirit of our age, looks at humanity. His gaze is full of longing for people to turn and look towards him. Why does the Archangel Michael, as the guardian of the conscience of the times, have such a high level of concern for humanity today? We are living in an age in which the image of the Son of Man wants to appear in the clouds of heaven. The time of a new closeness to Christ has arrived, and Michael's concern is that people will be completely oblivious to the mystery of their age. Will their conscience not be stirred? Will at least a few notice what is happening above them and elevate their gaze?

*

The task of The Christian Community is not simply to cultivate a religious mood. We began our work in 1922 when Rudolf Steiner proclaimed anew, in a form appropriate for modern consciousness, knowledge of the higher worlds. From the outset, thanks to his godparenting of a new spiritual understanding, a prophetic element has lived among us. The foreknowledge with which we set out on our path included an apocalyptic premonition. We knew from Steiner that from 1933 onwards a significant Christ event would unfold, and since we knew about the approach of the light, we were also prepared for its shadow. How did it all play out?

People were excited at first. They had a dim feeling that something big was about to happen, but they knew nothing of a higher world and focussed only on the political situation. They succumbed to the demonic seduction emanating from the counterimages and caricatures of what was really happening. It was not just some megalomaniacal personality who appeared in the figure of Adolf Hitler. He could not have appeared at all if the demonic shadow had not fallen on his soul, and this only occurs when the organs for perceiving a great spiritual event have withered and died out. Thus, caricatures and distortions of what happens in the heavens appear in our age as earthly history. In 1933 very few people were aware of what was really happening above us!

We enter the future knowing that the drama's trials and culmination at the end of the century are imminent. Until the end of the century, humanity still has time to decide. And even if only a small group decides, the final disaster can be averted. It is not as if it were possible to avoid external catastrophes. But the real disaster would be that Christ comes and humanity renounces him by not seeing him in the moment of his coming. It was already like that when Christ walked the earth as a human being. He was there, yet those who had spoken so much about the Messiah did not recognise him. He did not come as they had imagined him, and so they crucified the one who was their Messiah.

Today, the material level completely dominates our thinking, while the world in which Christ approaches – indeed, in which he already is – is denied. This is a denial of Christ himself, even if one counts oneself a Christian. The denial of the spiritual world today is a battle against Christ, regardless of whether it comes

12. CHRISTIANS AND THE CONSCIENCE OF THE TIMES

from the churches or other circles. That is the severity of the crisis we are dealing with today.

Great hopes haunt the human soul, but it would be wrong to cherish only those hopes that focus on the world around us. How easily we are disappointed! Space travel to the moon, if not Mars, seems within reach. However, the question is whether such hopes do not lead to the greatest disappointments precisely when fulfilled. Shouldn't we say, what good is it for human beings if they can travel to the moon and can't even find their way back to themselves? Instead, we turn our gaze back to coarse, earthly things. A false view, a distorted perspective, means that instead of looking up to the heavens and taking part in the full scope of the events of our time, we are always fascinated by political or technical things. And this leads people to be blinded by illusions. Humanity should direct its gaze to where the real events of our time are taking place: up and over the 'clouds of the heavens'. Rather, our gaze is diverted by illusion. Today, humanity should learn to work with supersensible spiritual power and energy. We should mature to discover a higher world's etheric vitality and healing power and channel it into human work and our life together. At that exact moment, however, we are distracted by the prospect of interplanetary travel and the achievements of the nuclear industry.

Not the slightest thing should be said against what is happening in the technical or political fields. However, what is being achieved can only be beneficial if at least some people listen to the true conscience of the times and realise that these are caricatures of spiritual realities. For example, space travel is a caricature of our need to find our inward ascent to the supersensible world. Michael's most urgent concern is that we see through such distracting manoeuvres.

What this spirit of our age wants to do for us is to reawaken in us our sleeping powers of conscience. Under a new worldview, which shows us which fellow knowers wish to accompany the human soul, the powers of conscience become powers of vision. Seeing Christ does not take place with our physical eyes. However, it will not happen with miraculous clairvoyance either. It will happen when the moral aspect of human beings, their heart and conscience, become their eye. When the perception of Christ in the etheric begins in humanity – and the beginnings of this are already happening today – what the world above us is waiting for will finally occur. God is looking at people, seeing whether they realise and turn around so their eyes meet. This turning around, this changing of our minds and our heart's transformation, which enables it to perceive through conscience, is what can transform the disappointment of the angels into joy and satisfaction. When the conscience of the times opens its eyes within us, we stand face to face with Christ himself.

13

Progressive Christianity

(1955)

A restless mood has taken hold of humanity today, causing it to rush from one great advance to another, but at such a relentless pace it will not be possible for us to keep up with the progress we have made. It is tragic that Christianity, which should be placing the most critical inner values on the other side of the scales, is not itself keeping up with the rapid changes, believing instead that it can satisfy the new age with outdated forms. Honest self-reflection in these times leads us to the conclusion that in the field of religious life, not only is there no progress, but there is in fact regression. Even in the days of Swabian theologians Johann Albrecht Bengel and Christoph Friedrich Oetinger, piety was of a much warmer and more radiant character than is found in religious circles today. The progress of civilisation is of a cold nature, and the cold wind of modern life threatens the last remnants of religious warmth. Outwardly, our world is developing magnificently, but inwardly, love and devotion are dying of cold.

In this disparity between society's outward advances and the lagging behind of its religious life, we can already see the secular principle encroaching on the domain of religion. In earlier times, for example, it was often the case that the houses in which people lived received their architectural style from sacred buildings, from church architecture. Today, it is the other way around: places of worship take their architecture from railway stations and department stores. Instead of progress in Christianity, there is a secularisation, a profanation of religion.

A hundred years ago, when all this was still in its infancy, the Romantic poet Justinus Kerner wrote his poem 'In the Railway Yard':

> Go on, O man! Push it to the limit
> From steamship to ship of the air!
> Fly with the eagle, fly with the lightning
> We won't get further than the grave.[1]

Since the beginning of the twentieth century, people have gradually become numb to what is going on around them in daily life. Hardly anyone, it seems, is shocked by the number of road deaths. Today, civilisation takes the 'tomb' for granted. When we say of certain motorbike or car drivers that they drive like the devil, that is not without a grain of truth. A cold obsession has entered the civilised world. It is as if an invisible figure has hypnotised humanity and is cracking the whip. Of course, no one who is against development and not a lover of even the most modern progressiveness can join in the conversation. Yet it is necessary to see through the fact that since the beginning of the twentieth century, the sudden mass use of electricity, the automobile and all the other modern achievements that have entirely changed the face of the world have brought about an internal change in the climate of human life. People have not simply continued in the materialistic culture. The materialism on which the second half of the nineteenth century prided itself, its crude affirmation of earthly matter, its sheer worldliness, has come to an end. Even though today's atomic researchers say that materialism has already outlived its scientific usefulness, people's materialistic attitude is not decreasing but becoming more blatant.

It is nevertheless true, however, that humanity has left behind materialism. For example, atomic energy is what is released when matter decays, but when matter decays it does not disintegrate into something material; instead the gates of the subsensible are opened. A humanity that is reluctant to strive for a worldview that grasps the supersensible is, to a tremendous extent, already working with the subsensible. There is not only a 'beyond' upwards but also a 'beyond' downwards. Where do the enormous energies released during nuclear fission in the nuclear industry come from?

Once upon a time, our entire universe and our existence on earth was brought into being by the immeasurable cosmic energies of divine worlds. Today, creation has grown old and is begin-

13. PROGRESSIVE CHRISTIANITY

ning to die and decay, and now humanity is helping this process of death and decay through the violent thrusts of its progressive work. Thus, the same cosmic forces that created the world emerge again, to an extent, as forces of destruction from below. We no longer live in creation; we live in anti-creation.

This extends to the seemingly harmless field of synthetics. For what do we actually have in things like nylon and foam material? If we look at the raw materials, we realise that the forces of the abyss are already at work here as well. Many of these substances are produced from toxic natural gases, such as acetylene and hydrocyanic acid, so their very production is a constant danger to life. Gas masks have to be used. With the gifts of the abyss, the great miracle of producing indestructible materials has been achieved.

Alarming problems accompany both the nuclear and synthetics industries. What do we do with the nuclear waste, the radioactive substances that remain? They poison our planet because they do not lose their radioactivity. And what do we do with synthetic waste once the items made from it are no longer usable? They don't decompose, so they can't be left to the earth to turn back into soil. It is all made to last forever. Why? Because we are working with death, with the final deadness of earthly matter – that is, with the forces of the abyss. One day, we will no longer know what to do with these things because they will make the ground on which they are poured barren.

Since the beginning of the twentieth century, we have penetrated into subterranean, sub-earthly regions of creation. An image from the Revelation to John belongs here. It speaks of the angel who has the key to the bottomless pit. After a thousand years have passed, he unlocks the abyss, and the satanic power in chains begins to stir, becoming free and active.

Until now, people have used the idea of the Millennial Kingdom in an illusory sense. People have thought that the Millennial Kingdom is the golden age of peace and prosperity that will one day come. In reality, the Millennial Kingdom refers to the period of grace that humanity is given repeatedly in the course of its development so that it might test the powers it has cultivated and thereby acquire them permanently. In our time, such a Millennial Kingdom has come to an end. The lull is over. The powers of the abyss will now spread throughout our culture and will operate tyrannically in a perfectly respectable seeming manner. We only fail to understand that because our ideas of the opposing powers are too naive. Although our age is still more inclined to believe in the devil than in angels, we have no idea what kind of satanic power exercises dominion over the forces of the abyss because we only understand the devil to be a moral seducer. Here, we are dealing with an impersonal power that utilises the cold cleverness of human thinking. The lower realm of the beyond enters human culture from these sources.

However, the lower gates would not have opened in our century if gates had not also burst open above our heads. For it is never the case that the gates of hell open one day and only those of heaven the next: either humanity stands before closed gates above and below, or both sets are opened and we are caught in the conflict being waged for humanity between the powers above and the powers below.

Certain trivial sectarian views have turned the concept of the Second Coming of Christ into something that an educated person no longer wants to hear about. It is out of the question that the 'return of Christ' will occur as an event on the physical plane. In this field, people have lost themselves in illusions that stem from religious egotism. This is because Christianity has long since reached the point where it makes no distinction between Jesus and Christ. We only know the man Jesus; we do not know the divine being who became human through him and whom we call Christ. We cannot speak of a return of Jesus, but we can speak of a new revelation of Christ. This future mystery of Christianity is beginning to unfold in our time, and we must change the way we are accustomed to thinking and expand our ideas and concepts if we wish to understand this.

The name Christ designates a being who is the creative element in the universe. Even before entering earthly incarnation, he had gone through heavenly destinies of immense significance and then he passed through death and resurrection. When the disciples encountered the Risen One during the forty days after Easter, they might have thought that this was a figure like that of Jesus of Nazareth, who had been in their midst for three years.

13. PROGRESSIVE CHRISTIANITY

But it was indeed the Risen One. He remained in close proximity to the disciples for forty days until they witnessed how this being poured himself out, not into an otherworldly heaven, but into the entire etheric life of our earthly existence. It was only because he grew beyond the perceptive capacity of the disciples that Christ seemed to disappear from them. The Bible never refers to the renewed presence of Christ as a 'return', rather it uses the word *parousia*, which means 'being present'. This presence then undergoes an intensification such that it will become possible for humanity to have a new experience of Christ.

When it says that Christ will come 'on the clouds of heaven', we can understand this image in the following way. When the earth's atmosphere is saturated with the moisture that collects in the clouds, the water that moistens the earth and makes it fertile flows out of the clouds. Even if this is only a rough comparison, something similar happens in the progressive destiny of the Christ being. His being poured itself out into the etheric realm of the earth and grew into it with an ever-greater intensity. This will become so great that from the clouds of the etheric realm, Christ's power will reach us as mightily as does the rain from the clouds in the sky. The biblical writings describe such an event as the *parousia*, the coming of Christ. It is a tremendous evolutionary step, not of the man Jesus, but of the divine essence of Christ, and our time should experience something of it.

Because our eyes are blind to the supersensible world, we do not perceive the real-world events that pass through the spiritual spheres above our heads. True world history happens above. Otherwise, the Lord's Prayer would not say, 'Thy will be done, on earth as it is in the heavens.' Something is happening above our heads: a new coming, a new closeness of Christ to humanity is occurring. Tragically, for the time being, people only experience the shadow of this, the opening of the abyss. Thick clouds obscure his light and people's vision is too weak to penetrate them. That is why the progress of Christianity does not match the progress of external civilisation. But Christ himself is advancing. In the times ahead, the advancing Christ will become known to more people; Damascus-like experiences will pervade individual souls like sheet lightning, and the scales will fall from their eyes so that they can see what is really going on.

But how does the Christian religion, which is cultivated on earth, relate to the progress of Christ? Two thousand years ago, people looked up to heaven expecting the Messiah, and they were blind to the simple man Jesus, in whom the Messiah was incarnated. They misjudged him and crucified him. In our time, people are fascinated by the material realm, while in the spiritual realm, the one who alone can give meaning to our future and bring about real progress in humanity is passing by above our heads.

But there are already fruits of Christ's new closeness. Rudolf Steiner's life work is a testimony to the fact that one human being achieved a view of what is happening above our heads. The emergence of The Christian Community is also an effect of Christ, who has come near again. How could we, as a small circle of predominantly young people, have dared to establish a new priesthood, build altars and administer sacraments if we had not really experienced our mission to give the Christian religion a form corresponding to what can be read from the spiritual facts today?

Tradition has always known that the Antichrist will reveal himself in a particular way before Christ comes again. Christ will not come in an age of paradisal peace, but in a time of storms and tempests. The new coming of Christ falls in the period of our greatest remoteness from God. The satanic power emerges from the abyss and people use the gifts of the abyss as if nothing were wrong. In this, the Antichrist has the upper hand. The gifts of the abyss are given out easily, and humanity does not need to make any sacrifices to acquire them. But in the end, they have nothing of any real substance to offer human beings.

Christ cannot give us his gifts from the outside. We can only receive them out of our innermost freedom. Because of this, today's humanity is still estranged and distant from heaven's gifts, which are waiting for us in abundance. All that remains is the hope that people will eventually become wise through suffering.

Human health has deteriorated the more modern civilisation has cut us off from nature. But we have not only lost nature, we have also begun to deal with sub-nature, with the gifts of

13. PROGRESSIVE CHRISTIANITY

the abyss, as a matter of course in everyday life. Undoubtedly, we have become ill simply by working with electricity, let alone radioactivity. General nervousness is only the initial stage of a general civilisational disease. But the miracle drugs that people are so proud of today cannot truly cure this illness; they can only eliminate the disease's symptoms. The gifts of the abyss, even in the form of medication, only make people sicker. Indeed, one could say that if Satan were wholly free from the chains that have kept him locked in the abyss, everyone would already be quite ill. Will these setbacks eventually bring people to their senses? If a religious life could receive the gifts of Christ that are even now appearing above our heads, it would lead to a healing that reaches right down into the body. A world of life and power has drawn near that can heal souls and renew all areas of culture.

Two things are necessary. First, to help us in our struggle with the powers of the abyss, we must develop what Paul calls 'the art of discerning spirits'. Second, we must endeavour to experience the returning Christ. Seeing Christ and seeing through the Antichrist are the two tasks facing contemporary Christianity. To do this we must take to heart the words of Christ to his disciples in Gethsemane: 'Stay awake and pray' (Matt. 26:42).

Part of 'staying awake', waking up from the sleep of illusions and the influence of the abyss, is learning to look at the development of recent decades somewhat differently. The meaning of everything that happens on earth is found in the spiritual world above; what occurs below is merely a reflection. Take, for example, the youth movement, which existed before the outbreak of the First World War. A rising light was already active in the spiritual realm from which, although they did not perceive it as such, the young people were able to draw new ideas for humanity's future. A genuinely Christian impulse was at work within the youth movement's first attempts, even if Christ's name was not mentioned. To a certain extent the same also applies to the emergence of the labour and women's rights movements, even if they were concerned with entirely different life problems. Rays of light shone through here and there, but because they did not penetrate consciousness, they quickly darkened and were soon overwhelmed by the shadows of the great wars.

The small circle that set out to found The Christian Community after the First World War felt a special bond with all those friends who had died in large numbers on the battlefields. Their youthful idealism remained with us as a Christian impulse. Then came 1933. Those of us in The Christian Community, together with all those who had listened to Rudolf Steiner, knew very well that the year 1933 would mark a special stage in the developments taking place above our heads. We were not unprepared for what was to come, but what did come next? Although a vague presentiment about the future ran through humanity in Central Europe, people were blind to what it really meant and in the end they focused this feeling on the most inappropriate figure. A mighty cosmic being had appeared in the spiritual realm, but rather than looking up, people looked down at the caricature that had appeared in Adolf Hitler. If they had only perceived the reality, they would have seen through the caricature and not fallen for it.

When the war ended, people affected by the tremendous losses in Central Europe felt something of the true meaning of history. In the face of the horrors of the war, the question 'What is the human being?' was asked with repeated urgency, and there was a fierce debate about what it meant to be a human being. As everything lay in ruins, people were inclined to ask searching, inner questions – at least for a while. Minds were open, and many souls perceived, albeit indistinctly, something of the image of the human being: the Son of Man in the clouds of heaven. This all passed through people's feeling life, but soon the frenzy of reconstruction drew a curtain in front of the light that souls had sensed, and questions about the human being ceased to be asked. Today, we can only speak of hopeless confusion and paralysing disappointments.

What we are talking about here lies on a different level. If we could rise to that level, we would be able to recognise what is a worthwhile hope and what is already becoming a disappointment. Nor would we be lulled to sleep by any temporary economic miracle. We cannot rebuild and save a culture pregnant with doom with the same forces that were the cause of its misfortune and downfall. We have learnt nothing from these events.

But why do the great cataclysms of humanity happen if not to call people to change their thinking? Today it is unnecessary

13. PROGRESSIVE CHRISTIANITY

for someone to appear who, like John the Baptist at the time of Christ, says, 'Change your hearts and minds.' It is almost palpable that a spiritual world above and its shadowy counterpart below want to intervene in humanity in the battle for our souls.

Among Christ's entourage is a powerful, forward-looking spirit who inspires our present age: the Archangel Michael. He is concerned with humanity's progress and wants to drive us forward, but in an inwardly understood way. Our whole feverish drive for progress in outer areas comes from us confusing the light with its shadow. We can only understand many of today's events if we take them as silhouettes of what is really happening.

In the past, the purpose of religious life was, essentially, to live in such a way that one would go to heaven when one died. Such a childish longing for heaven has now been replaced by the caricatured idea of travelling to the moon and Mars. This is the form of spiritual longing, deeply chilled in the icebox of materialism, that flashes through our age. Working with the atom means reaching into a world beyond space, where space no longer prevails. The spiritual is of a supra-spatial nature. The ability to travel beyond the speed of sound is an endeavour to collapse time. And how does that affect people? In the caricature that no one has time any more. We have the desire to strive beyond space and time to reach the spirit – we are indeed looking for a true spiritual world – but all that remains is a distorted caricature. Instead of experiencing eternity, we merely have 'no time'.

Today, it is essential to cultivate a form of Christian life in which we can find the connection with Christ in the clouds as he reveals himself anew, while at the same time remaining a person of the present. We do not need to prudishly condemn our present achievements; everything should serve the future. However, the more external progress we make, the more this must be balanced by an inner progress. The Christian Community wants to contribute to this by cultivating a contemporary sacramental life. True worship is the school in which the soul practises upward openness. The striving upwards from below, which characterised the piety of Protestantism, leads in the long run to cramping human beings so that what is already hovering above them only finds an ever more difficult entrance into their souls. We want to cultivate a sphere of devotion at our altars in which people learn to leave all their nervousness outside and make themselves completely open to the presence of God, the ever-presence of Christ himself. Christ is here. He is present above our heads and has no greater longing than for people to open themselves to him. When people open themselves up to him, he is with them and in them. At a time when both the gates of the abyss and heaven are open, The Christian Community wants to serve humanity through a culture of knowing devotion, wakefulness and prayer.

14

Michael's Transformations
(1948)

The sun: is it nothing more than a luminous ball of fire out there in space? It has a gigantic yet measurable circumference, and our earth orbits it at an even more gigantic but measurable distance. Yet the star that circles our sky is only a sign indicating an all-encompassing, all-pervading being. It is the visible heart of a tremendous spherical entity that is not visible to our eyes. Certainly, as a life-giving power, the sun cannot be identical to that ball of fire. If it were nothing but its physical radiations of light and heat, then only desiccation and death could emanate from it, as we see in the earth's desert climates.

The ancient mythical consciousness of humanity still saw through the solar star as if through a window into its multi-layered, hierarchical, spherically graded essence. Thus, the Greeks saw the circling daylight as the vehicle of a god, as Helios's chariot, but above and behind Helios they worshipped a higher deity: Apollo, whom they called Phoebus, the 'Shining One'. What we see with our eyes points us towards the sphere of Helios, but the sphere of Phoebus Apollo is of a higher, supersensible nature. Apollo is the lord of spiritual sunlight and, with his harp, also the lord of the divine harmonies of the spheres, which have their source and centre in the sun, as Goethe writes:

> The day-star, sonorous as of old,
> Goes his predestined way along,
> And round his path is thunder rolled,
> While sister-spheres join rival son.[1]

When the ancients turned to Apollo, they felt the sun's immense etheric body pulsating throughout our universe with life. Yet behind Apollo, the ancient mystery centres recognised even higher divine beings, members of the all-embracing sun being. This ancient knowledge still resonated in Christian times, especially in the teachings on the threefold sun by the fourth-century philosopher-emperor Julian the Apostate.

The highest spiritual being of the sun, the sun's actual self, was proclaimed by Zarathustra as Ahura Mazdao, the sublime solar aura. This solar spirit was the god destined to pass through death and resurrection and whom later pre-Christian religions, longing for his advent, worshipped as Osiris and Adonis, as well as under many other names. Early Christianity still retained the idea that this supreme solar spirit had lived in Christ as a man among men, but by the time of Julian, this mystery had already been forgotten.

The writers of the New Testament still took for granted knowledge of the angelic hierarchies. Going back to Dionysius the Areopagite, St Paul's great Athenian disciple, this elaborate doctrine was carried into the high Middle Ages along with an ancient solar wisdom that flowed into Christianity. What the ancient world had experienced in direct vision was preserved in the feeling that the sun is the gate or window through which a supreme divine being looks at us from hierarchically organised spheres. It speaks to us from every level of the spiritual world through the beings who are its sheaths and messengers there. The hierarchies were arranged in coloured circles as if they formed an immense spiritual aura hidden behind the physical sunlight. Numerous paintings bear witness to this, such as the one in the cupola of the Baptistery next to Florence Cathedral.

It is not only the case that the divine realms look at us through the eye of the sun. We, too, can look into that realm when we penetrate its blinding outer appearance. That is why the Archangel Michael always plays a special role whenever the angelic hierarchy is mentioned. Michael is described as the prince of the hierarchies, the archangel of the sun, who appears from behind the light of day as a spiritual figure close to the human level. But he is only the countenance of higher realms of existence, members of Christ's body, and therefore of Christ himself.

The countenance of a human being is not their essence. It is a part of their bodily sheath, though it is more expressive than the rest of the body so that the 'I' can reveal itself through it. Like-

14. MICHAEL'S TRANSFORMATIONS

wise, Michael is the countenance of the spiritual world's entire hierarchy and, most of all, the countenance of Christ.

At the climax of its dramatic narrative, the Revelation to John shows us Michael as the victor over the dragon. The battle with the dragon has appeared as a basic mythical image at all stages of human spiritual history. In pre-Christian times, exalted figures carried out that battle with the enemy: in Babylon, he was called Marduk; among the Indians, Indra, and among the Greeks, it was Apollo who threw the dragon, Python, into the Castalian Gorge. During early Christianity, the Persian cult of the divine sun hero, Mithras, spread across the entire Mediterranean region. In Christian times, more human champions defeated the dragon: Siegfried on Nordic soil, which had not yet been taken over by Christianity, and St George among the early Christian saints. Is the conqueror of the beast always the same, only with changing names, be they divine or human?

A hierarchical mystery connects the various victors. The triumph over the dragon appears on all levels of the spiritual realms. In pre-Christian times, beings above the archangel level – Marduk, Indra, Apollo – appear in that image. They appear, so to speak, through the transparency of the Michael figure, who is a countenance between above and below. Following the Christ event, people who stood out from the general human realm through their spiritual power became transparent for the figure of the Archangel Michael who worked through them, among them the last Nordic initiate, Siegfried, and the first Christian knight, St George. Michael's metamorphoses appear on all rungs of the celestial ladder due to the world's transparency, which prevails in the spiritual realm of the sun.

In the image of victoriously conquering the dragon, we have a sun mystery and, at the same time, a mystery of the spiritual human being. Just as the plant derives its power from the sun to rise upright and face the sky, we owe our upright form, which enables us to triumph over all that is inferior, to the spiritual sun forces. As human beings we are inwardly related to the sun. We rise above the animal, which remains banished to the forces of the earth's depths simply because it lacks an upright form.

Overcoming the beast outwardly in our bodies formed part of our earlier development. Overcoming the beast inwardly in our souls is an ongoing moral goal for the future. That is the meaning of the mythical image of fighting the dragon.

First, higher divine beings are the victors over the dragon. We see the solar powers at work, creating human beings through great cosmic stages. There are descriptions by Rudolf Steiner that relate the image of Michael's battle with the dragon to the creation of the earthly animal kingdom. The spiritual guiding powers held humanity back in the spiritual realm, waiting for the right time for us to enter earthly embodiment. They had to defend us against adversaries who did not want to wait and instead pushed for embodiment. These adversaries were cast down to earth and the first fruits of the earthly animal kingdom emerged before the physically embodied human being existed. At each evolutionary stage, the battle with the dragon takes place, coming ever closer to the earthly level. It ends with the dragon being overthrown. That always happens to protect the developing spiritual human being, who, through all degradations and distortions, is to be shaped according to the highest sun-like divine archetype. After all, the highest Lord of the sun, the true God of humanity who bears the human archetype in his being, has himself entered earthly embodiment to snatch fallen human beings from the dragon powers of the depths.

In Christian times, the human metamorphoses of Michael emerged as dragon conquerors. This indicates that the future of human beings as spiritual beings, threatened by demonic powers, is now in our own hands. Especially in our apocalyptic present, human sun-warriors are to be counted upon. The servants of Christ who meet the spiritual demands of the time are those who are, in the Michaelic sense, fellow fighters with Michael.

15

Michael, the Prince of Progress
(1956)

One being who does not stand still is the Archangel Michael. The childlike images that earlier centuries painted of the one who vanquishes the dragon can tell us much, but they do not show us the archangel in his present form, nor do they allow us to feel his current sense of urgency. When he last guided humanity on a large scale it was in the centuries before the incarnation of Christ, during the time of Alexander the Great's conquests. Now, in our time, Michael's whole gesture has undergone a transformation. His hand, which in that earlier age was outstretched in a militant manner against the forces of the enemy, now beckons to us in freedom. Michael is the prince of progress, which is to be achieved through the free deeds of human beings who respond to his silent gesture.

In this lies Michael's infinite closeness to Christ. The traditional conception of the divine sees the divinity as eternally immutable. From this, people believe they should derive unchanging religious traditions and forms. It is undoubtedly possible to grasp something of the Father God's essence, the divine ground of the world, through such an idea. However, it does not allow a feeling for the essence of Christianity to emerge.

Christ, the Son, is not immutable. He is the being who brings about all evolution in the world, all growth and development. From the beginning, he has been on a great journey of all-encompassing transformation. Even before the event of Golgotha, he had repeatedly given the ages their new character by wandering from sphere to sphere towards earthly humanity. And even after the three years of becoming fully human, he did not remain, as is believed, in the ascended state he entered on the fortieth day after Easter. The image of him ascending into heaven only indicates that a further development has begun. The question we should therefore ask is, 'Where is Christ, and how does he work today?'

The significant trait of ceaseless, forward-striving progress, which characterises the Christ being, becomes clearer and more familiar when we succeed in forming a picture of the present-day figure of the Archangel Michael. Just as John the Baptist did two thousand years ago on the earthly plane, Michael today paves the way for Christ in the spiritual world closest to humanity. It is the dynamic nature of the Christ that determines the nature of the one who, clearing all obstacles from his path, precedes him.

That part of Michael's life during which he stood before the Father God is richly reflected in the Old Testament. From the book of the prophet Daniel, we learn that until the Babylonian exile Michael was the inspiring spirit of the Israelite-Jewish people (Dan. 10:13 and 21). Through Michael's inspiring guidance, the inner history of this people could be seen as the earthly equivalent of Christ's progress in the supersensible worlds at that time.

It was Michael's leadership that made the people of the Old Covenant the 'chosen people'. The focus of human development lay with them for hundreds of years. As its vanguard, they had to achieve a level of development on behalf of humanity that would offer the possibility for Christ to incarnate. They had to develop a certain soul power that would, one day, allow all of humanity to fully and freely grasp the working of Christ.

Just as the earthly path of Christ had to lead to Golgotha, the place of the skull, humanity's inner development had to lead to the place of the skull, even if that entailed much impoverishment and inner death. For the sake of humanity, the 'chosen people' had to acquire a thinking that is bound to the head and brain. It makes us poor, but it also makes us free. Although Michael is the archangel of the sun, when Christ in his pre-earthly existence sent him forth as a herald, he had to become the spiritual leader of a people whose mission was a lunar one: namely to develop the lunar powers of reflective thought for humanity. The light of the spiritual sun, which was already rising – the sunlight of the Christ being – could not yet appear directly to humanity. Human nature was not ready for this; it was still too soft and nebulous.

For a time, therefore, it fell to the Israelite-Jewish people, as the 'chosen people' of humanity, to reflect the approaching sunlight through the lunar forces in their souls. The moon itself does not shine, but when the sun is below the horizon, the moon reflects the sunlight like a mirror. Humanity received Christ's sunlight through a reduced lunar reflection. They learnt to think with a thinking bound to the brain. The type of thoughts our brains can carry are reflections of the great divine thoughts, just as moonlight, is reflected sunlight. We also say that we 'reflect' with our minds. In fact, we reflect world reason. Our brains form reflections and shadow images of the divine world's ideas.

Instead of saying that Michael stood before the Father God at that time, we can also say that he was the countenance of Yahweh before he became the countenance of Christ. Yahweh is a being whom we can visualise in the image of the moon, just as the sun is the true image of Christ. Paradoxical as it may seem, the sun archangel became the countenance of a lunar deity so that, when the time was fulfilled, he could become the countenance of the spiritual sun, the Christ being.

There is a reason why humanity today is so far removed from an accurate understanding of Michael's nature. We see history essentially as a sequence of external events, such as the change in global power relations and the successes and failures of human endeavours. We have not yet realised that a crucial aspect of human development involves the evolution of consciousness. The Archangel Michael is humanity's guide and inspirer on its journey through the various transformations of consciousness. According to Rudolf Steiner, Michael is the 'administrator of the cosmic intelligence', and it is precisely in this that he is the most direct hierarchical servant and forerunner of Christ.[1]

The great Greek thinkers from Heraclitus to the Stoics already knew of Christ and, like the Old Testament prophets, foresaw his coming. They called him the 'Logos', just as the evangelist John did at the beginning of his gospel. Logos does not simply mean 'Word'. Rather, it points to that exalted sphere of origin wherein God's thinking and speaking are one. In the primal beginnings, Christ's garment or spiritual corporeality consisted of the original, creative thoughts of God. We can call these thoughts 'world reason' or 'cosmic intelligence'. The spiritual sun, Christ, of which the sun of the outer firmament is only a symbol, consists of God's luminous thoughts, and Michael is the herald and helper of the Logos. He ensures that what is right always happens on successive world levels so that world reason can shine directly into the human spirit.

A critical stage on that path occurred when, stimulated by Moses, sense-bound intellectual thinking took shape in the Israelite-Jewish people. The lunar imprint of world reason emerged as the sun archangel bowed in service to the moon: the gold spirit minted silver coins. Michael undertook this task because it is only by passing through the shadowy head intelligence that human beings are able to develop an ego, a self that is able subsequently to be the independent producer of an elevated thinking. Yahweh's mission was necessary for preparing Christ's mission, and so Michael was the countenance of Yahweh before he could become the countenance of Christ.

Folk history ends for the Old Testament stream when, following the Assyrian destruction of the kingdom of Israel's ten tribes, Judah's kingdom, with its remaining two tribes, was also destroyed at the time of the Babylonian captivity. Yahweh's mission had come to an end, and this allowed Michael to free himself from his ties to the Hebrew people and rise from folk spirit to time spirit. A Michael age began in which Michael's solar character could appear more directly. This found expression even in the lunar nature of the Hebrew people. Messianic prophecies dominated the proclamations of their prophets as the first rays of Christ's coming became visible from afar: a new day was about to dawn.

During this time, Michael's inspiration reached all over the world. In Greece, the great thinkers from Pythagoras to Plato and Aristotle were contemporaries of the prophets, along with the great Buddha in India, Zoroaster in Persia, and Lao Tzu and Confucius in China. The gathering of spirits extending across the whole earth was like a messianic dawn.

When the central event of earthly human history occurred, Christ's incarnation, death and resurrection, the Michael age had already ended. The heraldic torches that flared up everywhere had burnt out. The humanity's descending development had been arrested and was now being mercifully reversed. We must imagine the most intimate interweaving of the Archangel

15. MICHAEL, THE PRINCE OF PROGRESS

Michael with the events reported in the gospel. They do not describe it directly, but when lightning flashes through the quiet scenes of Galilee as if through a cloud, we see the countenance of Michael, who is so intimately involved in what is happening on earth.

The Archangel Michael once stood before the Father God; now, he stands before the Son God. He is the countenance of Christ and is preparing to become the countenance of humanity. The goal of this endeavour will be achieved when the sunlight of God's thoughts finally finds direct entry into human souls and are no longer darkened by mere sense-bound, head-bound thinking.

After the event of Golgotha, the Michaelic-Christ future flashes up periodically: for Paul before the gates of Damascus, and for John on Patmos, for example. But what a thick curtain the history of Christianity has since been able to weave in front of the light that already shines! For ordinary Christians, Christ's solar character was deeply veiled. They only saw the man Jesus. The idea that a relationship with Christ could also transform human consciousness was far removed. Christianity became increasingly accustomed to making a sharp distinction between faith and knowledge. Only in solitary seekers of God does the Michaelic longing for directly perceiving Christ arise.

In the service of Christ's future, Michael is increasingly working his way back into the dynamics of historical development. As in the Old Testament period, Michael is once again preparing to take on a folk. However, it would not be correct to say that Michael became the folk spirit of the German people. He hovered over the folk that formed in Central Europe but did not enter their blood with the same intensity and to the same degree as he had done with the Old Testament people. Thus, Michael's folk-soul impact on German spiritual history only ever appeared in individuals such as Fichte, Hegel, Schelling or Goethe. In them, thought wanted to break free from pale reflections and shadowy images. Through Michael's guidance, the whole of German spiritual history was preparing the ground for Christ's latest revelation, usually called the Second Coming. Only this time, rather than working towards Christ's physical birth, Michael is helping to create the spiritual conditions in that part of humanity which will be receptive to Christ's new coming.

THE AGE OF THE ARCHANGEL MICHAEL

The fact that in the second half of the nineteenth century, the bright Olympian thoughts of the Goethean age were extinguished and replaced by a more prosaic, everyday thinking, did not mean that Michael's influence was diminishing. By the end of the 1870s, contrary to outward appearances, Germany's national history had ended. Michael rose anew from his role as a folk spirit to his task as a time spirit. The German spirit was tasked with growing beyond national egoism in a selfless, comprehensive service to humanity.

In the current Michael age, which began in 1879, we have experienced the gigantic growth of the opposing powers and have had to endure their reports of triumph daily. This fundamentally increases the inner fear and distress of human souls who shudder in the face of what is to come.

But we have also already witnessed the beginnings of a new Michaelic inspiration. Michael's first great gift to our time was anthroposophy and the life work of Rudolf Steiner. If it dares to make this gift its own, humanity will be equipped with solar instead of merely lunar thoughts. Christ and Michael are close to us amid the growing stormy darkness; they bear the sun that shines at midnight. Without losing the strict, rigorous thinking that natural science has cultivated, we can find the transition from mere head-thinking to the creative Michaelic thoughts jointly conceived by head and heart. Therein lies the seed for beholding the supersensible and thus for the Damascus awakening of the human soul.

Michael has already triumphed in his battle with the dragon in the spiritual realm; now humanity, allied with Michael, the countenance of Christ, must achieve the same victory on earth. We do so not by fighting against what the powers of darkness have achieved through technological innovations, but through the positive spiritual power inherent in every Christ-like insight, every Christened thought.

Michael's gesture is no longer one of battle. He raises his hand and beckons to free human beings. If we choose to respond, then through all the horrors of the present time we can meet and serve the Easter Sun of the Risen One.

16
Christ and Michael
(1956)

Autumn is a time of testing. When the sun enters the constellation of Libra, the scales, at the end of September, humans are indeed weighed. Will their inner strength be sufficient when the nature that has supported them throughout the spring and summer months now withdraws and throws them back on themselves?

Today, we can speak of a lesser and a greater autumn. The lesser autumn is the one we experience every year, whereas the greater autumn is the age of the Archangel Michael, which humanity has entered on a larger scale. The greater autumn exercises its dominance after a summer era has come to an end, and intervenes in the yearly cycle by extending autumn's influence. Autumnal chills come earlier, meaning that almost no real, undisturbed summers are left.

The protective curtains that surrounded us through the warmth and beauty of nature's summer are suddenly pulled away as if by rough hands. A cold breeze buffets us, and stormy downpours thunder around us. But if we have the inner strength to stand firm, another figure emerges from the twilight's dim depths. In a light that shines mildly at first then ever more radiantly, the Archangel Michael steps forth. A golden glow emanates from his armour, and he holds the scales high in his hand. His mouth is closed. His earnest concerned eyes rest on us humans. His silent concern says, 'I am here for you; my whole endeavour is to help you. But if you remain as you are, I am not allowed to help you. Otherwise, you would still be what you are, and what you are is not enough for the world's future. First, you must become different; then, you will be sure of my help.'

We feel that this figure is not simply something outside of us; it concerns every one of us in our innermost being. He stands before us like a stern mirror of God and allows us to recognise how much we fail, how inwardly weak we are and, therefore, how we are always subject to the suggestion of merely external things.

Only when we honestly feel the seriousness of his testing does the archangel begin his teaching.

In the old legends that existed for every day of the year, the one relating to Michaelmas began with listing the nine angelic choirs. September 29 was called 'St Michael and all the Angels'. Our souls open to see the heavenly hierarchies from the angels and archangels up to the cherubim and seraphim. Michael stands before us as the representative and herald of the angelic realms and shows us all of them. The first thing he silently teaches us is to direct our gaze not only towards the realms of nature, but also towards the spirit realms. We must look beyond stone, plant, animal and humanity upwards to the seraphim; we must seek the true hierarchical greatness of existence.

And then everything begins to move. Like Faust, we see 'Celestial powers, who ever take and give vessels of gold on heaven's living stair,'[1] and feel like Jacob, who dreamt of a ladder to heaven: 'He had a dream in which he saw a stairway resting on the earth, with its top reaching to heaven, and the angels of God were ascending and descending on it' (Gen. 28:12).

What is this ascending and descending? What kind of conversation is this between heaven and earth that is not conducted with words but with reality?

Many religious people, caught up in the common worldview, want little to do with talk of angels and archangels. They are worried that the notion of hierarchical beings could demolish the great thought of God's unity. They do not want to stand before a multiplicity, but only before the sublime unity.

However, the sublime divine world unity appears to us when, following Michael's hint, we direct our gaze to the ascending and descending heavenly powers. They do not stop with the angels, but pass on their golden pails to humans, animals, plants and stones. The angelic hierarchies are all members of the body of the one God – and so are we, together with the entire earthly creation.

When we look back on our lives and say that we have felt the hand of God in our destiny, that is not just a figurative expression.

16. CHRIST AND MICHAEL

As protective and guiding spirits assigned to individual human beings, the angels are God's hands. We could call the archangels God's arms and the thrones God's feet. And Christ is God's heart. We sense the great unity. The ascending and descending movement within the multiplicity is like the pulsating flow, the living circulation of one great Being.

This divine circulation should also pass through human beings, but a tragic rupture in creation came about through the Fall. As a result, human beings dragged earthly creatures down with them into their separation from God. When we realise this, we begin to understand Michael's teaching: he wants to lead us from merely looking at separate outer nature to true self-knowledge and the perception of a new connection to the spiritual world. He wants his teaching to turn into an awakening.

In the great organism that encompasses heaven and earth, Michael has a specific function, one that makes him superior to the hierarchies above him, and which means he can be the herald and prince of all angels: he is 'the countenance of Christ'. What does this mean?

To all beings, Michael exemplifies a fundamental principle that connects all spheres, from the depths to the heights, and that is the principle of being open to what is above. Each level of being only fulfils its true nature by being open to the level above it: the angels must be open to the archangels, the archangels to the archai, and so on all the way up the ladder of being. Each level must be selfless enough to make itself an organ of the higher order; none must want to remain merely itself. In a superhuman way, Michael exemplifies the words of Paul in his Letter to the Galatians: 'Not I, but Christ in me' (Gal. 2:20). Michael too says, 'Christ in me,' and so Christ lives in him. Christ looks at us from Michael's eyes, Christ's thoughts shine from Michael's forehead, and if Michael were to open his earnest, silent mouth, Christ would speak through him.

This is what we mean when we say Michael is the countenance of Christ. In our time, it is important that we understand the mystery of true integration, of being 'within-one-another'. It no longer helps to imagine God and the angels and other higher beings as though they exist side by side or even facing each other.

If we think like this, we are more likely to end up waiting for a higher being, perhaps even God himself, to approach us from the outside and do something for us, whereas the actual law of our creation is a sublime and sacred 'within-one-another' – the law of indwelling.

We must learn to say as Paul did, 'Christ in me!', and when this is fulfilled, the Father will also live in us through Christ. The law of indwelling is the core principle of the Christian worldview.

People who want only to be themselves, sunk in their selfish and unreflecting behaviour, are never truly themselves. If we remain only what we are, we are not yet fully human. We only begin to be truly human when we are open to the inspiring spirit. Whether we speak of a person's angel or their true higher self, that is all just groping for the truth, but it is one the most important truths of our existence.

Vigilance is required here, however. While it is true that a person whose countenance does not shine with the radiance of an inspiring spirit is only a fragment or even a caricature of a human being, it is also true that when people make themselves open to a being who itself is not open to yet higher beings, then that being confers on them only a glittering, illusory brilliance. These people are not open in a truly selfless way. Their vanity and ambition draw into their soul a Luciferic and not a Christ-serving spirituality.

Human beings do not yet really have within themselves what is intended for them as their true essence. It still hovers over them. That is why they must connect with the choirs of angels who ascend and descend the heavenly ladder since the angels still carry and preserve human beings' true essence.

The principle of indwelling runs through all levels of existence where there is a selfless openness upwards. The being we call Christ has been the classic archetype and model of this openness since time immemorial. As described by spiritual research, Christ and Lucifer were brothers, belonging to the same hierarchical level. In the world's greater evolution, there came a moment when a being of that hierarchical rank had to be inclined to receive into himself the Logos, the Word of Worlds, whose sounding set our creation in motion. Christ was open upwards,

16. CHRIST AND MICHAEL

and the Logos, the Son principle, moved into him. Lucifer wanted to be himself and use the power of the Logos for his own ends. His selfish behaviour caused him to lose his rank and stability – he fell.[2] In the legends of many peoples, there is still a memory of Lucifer's fall, which occurred at the very moment when Christ was elevated to become the bearer of the Logos and, thus, the organ for the creation of our world.

The Christians of earlier eras always said in their services, 'The Lord be with you.' Today, we say, according to the Pauline-Christian principle of indwelling, 'Christ in you.' The old formula is not wrong, but it only applies to a childhood stage of humanity. You can say to a child, 'Your angel be with you.' Their guardian angel protects the child from danger, hovers over them at night and walks beside them by day. But when a person grows up, their relationship with their angel changes. Their angel releases them from its former care because that person is to become independent. Their angel no longer helps from outside without any action on their part.

The adult human being can only remain in contact with their angel if they take their angel in through a true openness to what lies above. That is the reason why we, having outgrown childhood, should not imagine Christ performing miracles for us from the outside. Only those who learn to say, 'Christ in me,' can count on his blessings. Christ's gifts want to be received inwardly, not passively, but through the active receptivity we call 'faith'.

We grow towards the fulfilment of a great Christian future when we accompany the words 'Christ in you' and 'Christ in us' spoken at the altar with an increasing inner activity of soul. They become guiding words of personal piety, and regular immersion in the sacramental life of the congregation and the prayer life of the individual support each individual's 'openness upwards'. Through the qualities of faith, hope and love, what is spoken at the altar comes to pass: Christ enters the human soul.

What happens when we begin to practise this is that our angel, who is the bearer of our higher self, moves into us. The more we permeate our earthly self with our higher self in this way, the more our angel becomes, so to speak, the 'countenance of Christ' for us. As the indwelling of Christ shines forth in our angel, it also takes place in ourselves.

This is the first stage, the stage of becoming a child of God, for which we must wrestle again and again in true filial devotion. The step from being a child of God to sonship then lies in the fact that not only our angel but now also the archangel, who is truly the 'countenance of Christ', begins to fill and permeate us. We experience the Archangel Michael's closeness and power and thus the closeness and power of Christ in a new way. A hint of this can always be seen when we feel urged not to keep the higher power awakening in us for ourselves but to actively display it in the service of the 'growing kingdom of God'. What first touched us in our feelings and made us quiet, filling our inner silence, wants to take hold of our will.

In his play *The Maid of Orleans*, Schiller wrote, 'Receive the deity into your will, and it will rise from its world throne.' Doesn't that sound to most Christians like impious audacity and presumptuous human arrogance? In reality, it shows that Schiller was aware of the Pauline-Christian principle of indwelling, even if he was probably not thinking of making a religious proclamation when he formulated the line. Here, he points to the mystery of indwelling in the Michaelic sense. Christ as the Logos, the Son, who includes human beings in his sonship, is the world's Creator. If we learn to speak and act in Christ's name, in the name of the Lord, then we may become bearers of a higher, grace-filled creative power.

It is not the case, however, that the Michaelic change in Christian attitudes comes about simply through stepping from feeling to will and action. The Archangel Michael is not so concerned with deeds of an external nature as with deeds of consciousness. He is the prince of evolution who wants to lead humanity from their blindness regarding the spiritual world to a new spiritual perception. Through our progressive fall into sin, the twilight of the gods dimmed humanity's old vision of God, but at the same time, we acquired freedom. Mere intellectual head consciousness is the midnight stage of humanity's broader evolution of consciousness. Today, Michael endeavours with all his might to lead human souls to a new sunrise.

16. CHRIST AND MICHAEL

That is why his interest is not in the will in general. Rather, Michael is more concerned with the will in thinking, which liberates our life from being merely brain-bound and permeates it with heart warmth. With the power of the whole human being, Michael releases thinking from its bondage to the sensory world and frees it for supersensible worlds.

The more we become familiar with the nature of Michael, the more directly will he appear to us as the countenance of the age that humanity has entered through the death and resurrection of Christ. He is the countenance of Christ, and because he is the countenance of Christ, Michael brings the indwelling of Christ to our consciousness. Michael allows Christ to dwell within himself so that in his perception, thinking and speaking, Christ himself sees, thinks and speaks. Michael clears the way in the souls of those who draw near to Christ so that Christ can see through our human eyes, think through our heads and speak through our mouths. The Christening of the heart is always the beginning of being a Christian, but Michael also wants the activity of our head, which bears our countenance, to be Christened.

Once upon a time, in humanity's historical development, the dividing line between faith and knowledge had to be drawn. For a time, heart and head went their separate ways for the development of consciousness. But the time when the coldness of the head opposed the warmth of the heart is over. Michael struggles for the Christening of thinking and knowing, and for the heart's participation in the activity of the head. We must wrest a Christianity of consciousness from humanity's autumn, in which our belief in knowledge and our discerning faith fully reconnect us to the angelic hierarchies, whose herald and prince is Michael.

If we say 'Christ in us' in the right way, Christ begins to dwell in our hearts.

When Michael says, 'Christ in me,' his countenance lights up as the countenance of Christ.

And when we say with Michael, 'Christ in us,' Christ works in our hearts and in our heads.

17.

The Spirit of Michael: Celebrating Transformation
(1957)

In our time, we must learn to find and feel anew that which is Michaelic. To do this we must look towards what is developing and must still be struggled for, for what is truly Michaelic never lies in what is complete and finished.

Forming an image of the Archangel Michael is not as easy as some might imagine. The images from earlier centuries no longer apply, and we must learn to find the Archangel Michael where he stands today, having left behind all his previous stages of activity. It is all too easy to form a ready-made, human-like image of him that distracts us from the elemental, all-pervading nature of Michael's work. Michael's spirit wants to be felt more like a wind that blows through the world, or perhaps even a storm that we must learn not to fear.

How does Michael communicate today? Michael's language is of a will nature, and although he is the archangel of the sun, he does not express himself through the spring and summer seasons, but through autumn. Michael does not whisper through the rising life of nature; he does not communicate through what can be given to us from the outside. He is not looking for mere recipients, people who only ever want to receive. He overlooks such people and looks instead for those who want to achieve their aims in and for the world.

Now, we are not only in the seasonal autumn, ushered in year after year by Michaelmas. We are also in a greater autumn, which gives our age its character because we have entered the age of Michael. It often seems as if the greater autumn of humanity causes the lesser, yearly autumn to come early. Increasingly, autumn seems to begin when it should still be summer, and so that aspect of autumn that demands steadfastness and inner

17. THE SPIRIT OF MICHAEL

activity from us will perhaps come more to the fore in the future. Perhaps it will also happen more often in the future that the beautiful autumn days will fail to appear. The world is becoming increasingly austere, and as sons and daughters of a Michael age we must find a more daring lifestyle.

Michael does not want to give us anything, nor does he want to spare us anything difficult. He does nothing to comfort us in life's difficulties. But it is not as if he is merciless and wants to torment us. When people face challenges that cause them great hardship, Michael says, 'You shall grow from this. Those who do not grow but break, who are too weak to pass the test of the greater autumn, will perhaps have their turn in a later life. But for now, I cannot work with them.'

We know this experience well. During the war, when we had to be prepared for air raids, as well as in the years immediately after, people were much more open and alive than they are now. During times of prosperity it is as though Michael is saying to us, 'If you are doing well, there is nothing I can do with you.'

Everything that comes to us from the outside, all good fortune and prosperity, too easily become obstacles to Michael's intentions. We do not make the proper use of these moments if we do not shift the focus of human existence inwards.

In summer, people go on holiday, travelling all around the world in search of rest and relaxation. In the future, however, we will realise that even at its most beautiful, nature will no longer help to restore our strength. Our depleted life forces will be refreshed and renewed only through inner recuperation, through inner activity and labour. In this way, the summer landscape is transferred to the inner soul, even if outwardly storms roar around us and the rain pours down. The inner summer landscape, created by the warmth of faithful inner practice, will give the person rest.

Michael always directs his gaze to the future. No matter how great the past may have been, or how much beauty nature may still preserve from its paradisal heritage, Michael's gaze does not focus on them. He knows they are in the process of decline. But he also knows that humanity must undergo all its trials and impoverishment for the sake of the future.

In fact, it is not even in Michael's interest to look back at what once happened as a historical event on Golgotha. He does not see the Mystery of Golgotha by looking back into history; rather, he sees it as something that is both present and future. That is why he wants to lead us to a new, higher awareness and understanding of Christ's life and his death on Golgotha, which continues to shine. For Michael, the event of Golgotha is, first and foremost, a key to the future. He wants it to be a principle of knowledge that every death properly died brings humanity forward, every suffering inwardly endured bears fruit. Thus, life continually blossoms out of death. Michael's silently spoken word says that the event of Golgotha is not something past, but a principle of life, a key to the future, and a focus of inner orientation for us. It is the content of his silent yet clearly audible call to our time.

How does Michael speak to us in the Bible? Here, too, he does not speak directly in human words; instead, we must approach the Bible as a dramatic whole, not simply select edifying individual verses.

When we think of the Old Testament, we often think of the historical books first. But then come the poetic books, including Psalms, and, finally, the prophetic books. At first, we have the naïve idea that all of this emerged from a single source of revelation. In the last one hundred and fifty to two hundred years, scholars have begun to claim that the Old Testament books were written down at very different times. But that quickly leads to losing God's word in the Bible, leaving only human words.

Let us take a look at the structure of the Old Testament, moving beyond the first two groups of books – the historical books and the poetic writings – to the third group, the prophetic books. In the prophetic books, our gaze is no longer directed towards the past as in the books of Moses, which look back to the creation of the earth, but towards the future. They are filled with prophecies of doom and salvation. Despite the catastrophes that befell the Hebrew people, the books of the prophets, especially that of the prophet Jeremiah, are full of warnings that more difficult times lie ahead, and that these are but the shadow of what is to come. Amid the storms, the prophets directed their gaze towards humanity's messianic future.

Since 1879, we have once more been in a Michael age. In the

17. THE SPIRIT OF MICHAEL

previous Michael age gigantic power blocs emerged, such as the Assyrian Empire and the Neo-Babylonian Empire in whose name Nebuchadnezzar smashed Judah and led the rest of the Israelite people into captivity.

Today, we also have great power blocs, which are now divided into East and West. Politically, Europe is sinking, and it will not become a major power if it does not take up its spiritual task. When a Michael age comes, national ties assume less significance. The national element, which people do not acquire for themselves but which they have through common descent, recedes into the background and a more cosmopolitan view of humanity comes to the fore. That was the case in the earlier Michael age, and it is so again today. National ambitions no longer work in a beneficial way since they are nothing more than a recourse to what has been. In a Michael age, the gifts of the past are no longer in keeping with the times. Now, with a Michaelic wind blowing through humanity, we feel the advent of a new spiritual element, and while it may offer us little in the way of comfort, nevertheless it addresses the innermost core of our being.

But what of the New Testament? Do we not find there something that corresponds to today's Michael age? In the New Testament we also have historical books – the gospels and the Acts of the Apostles – which look back on the three years of Christ's incarnation and the early Christian developments that immediately followed. These are then followed by Paul's letters and, right at the end, the Apocalypse of John. In the New Testament, we can easily feel that it all came out of a single revelation, especially since the fourth gospel and the Apocalypse come from the same John. But in those days, especially through the experiences of John on Patmos and Paul on the road to Damascus, provision was made for a time when humanity would again need prophetic books. This may seem paradoxical at first, but while the Pauline letters have existed for almost two thousand years, they were actually written for today. Likewise, the Apocalypse of John was recorded at the end of the first century, but it was written for our time. It is the scripture of our present Michael age.

The Apocalypse doesn't describe individual events for people to puzzle over and decipher; rather, it looks to the future as a whole. Certainly, we read the gospels with gratitude and reverence for what happened during the life of Christ. The name Jesus, the name of the man in whom Christ was embodied, tells us an inexhaustible amount. But when we mention the name of Christ, we are not thinking of someone that belongs to the past, but of the being who is alive in humanity today and on into the future. Not just the one who appeared two thousand years ago, but the one who will come in the future and who is already making his presence felt now. We look towards a messianic future, just as the Old Testament people in their Babylonian captivity looked towards the Messiah's coming.

This is Michael's way of speaking. The sun of Christ rises amid the destruction and trials that are meant to awaken and strengthen humanity inwardly. We are approaching a messianic future whose early stages have already begun. Yes, let us read the Bible! Let us hear the language of Michael, the language of apocalyptic consciousness, not in the individual words, but in the great dramatic structure of the New Testament!

We stand before the gate to a new nature, a new world of spring and summer rising amid the showers and storms of the present. The outer summer will become increasingly barren over the years, as the outer sun enters its descending arc. But they will be replaced by an inner summer and the radiance of an inner sun. Michael is the archangel of the sun, meaning the inner, spiritual sun. He confidently allows many things to become gloomier and colder, for his concern is that, with the return of Christ, a spiritual sun should rise in humanity. Around the altar, the flowers will bloom even in winter, the blossoms of the soul, the flowers in devotion's garden, and people will become healthy when they open themselves up to this summer splendour.

And so we want to look forward with great joyful expectation to what the future holds. The future will undoubtedly bring many horrors, but if we listen to Michael's apocalyptic language, it will also bring us a new closeness to Christ if only we venture out onto the stormy sea of change in this new age of Michael.

Notes

2. In the Age of Michael
1. See Steiner, *The Archangel Michael*, pp. 299–316.

3. Between Two Michael Ages
1. It isn't clear where Bock gets this figure from. At his trial before an ecclesiastical court in the Duchy of Brittany in October 1440, Gilles de Rais was accused of murdering more than 140 children. At the same time, he was tried by secular judges at the ducal court of justice for crimes against 'several small children'. He was hanged and burned at the stake on October 26, 1440. See https://en.wikipedia.org/wiki/Gilles_de_Rais.

4. Christian Ideals in the Age of Michael
1. Nietzsche, *Thus Spoke Zarathustra*.
2. Novalis, *Hymns to the Night*, at www.logopoeia.com/novalis/hymns.html#five.

6. The Confrontation with Evil
1. Schiller, Friedrich, 'Resignation' (1786). See: https://www.oxfordreference.com/display/10.1093/acref/9780191826719.001.0001/q-oro-ed4-00009175?p=emailAeXUSbaLKeuVY&d=/10.1093/acref/9780191826719.001.0001/q-oro-ed4-00009175
2. Goethe, *Faust: Part One*, pp. 41f.
3. Goethe, *Faust: Part Two*, pp. 27–38.
4. In *The Odyssey*, Homer replaces the sea monster with a massive whirlpool.

8. The World Situation and the True Spirit of the Times
1. Goethe, *Faust: Part One*, p. 50.

10. The Age of Light
1. Steiner, *Anthroposophical Leading Thoughts*, pp. 53f.

11. Michael and the New Coming of Christ
1. This is a phrase Rudolf Steiner often used to characterise the nature of the fall. See, for example, *Awake! For the Sake of the Future*, lectures of January 6 and 12, 1923.

13. Progressive Christianity
1. Kerner, Justinus, 'Im Eisenbahnhofe'. Available at: https://www.gedichte7.de/im-eisenbahnhofe.html.

14. Michael's Transformations
1. Goethe, *Faust: Part One*, p. 39.

15. Michael, the Prince of Progress
1. Steiner, *Karmic Relationships*, vol. 3, p. 133.

16. Christ and Michael
1. Goethe, *Faust: Part One*, p. 46.
2. See, for example, Steiner, *Man in the Light of Occultism*, lecture of June 12, 1912.

Bibliography

Goethe, Johann Wolfgang von, *Faust: Part One*, (tr. Philip Wayne), Penguin, UK 1949.
—, *Faust: Part Two*, (tr. Philip Wayne), Penguin, UK 1949.
Nietzsche, Friedrich, *Thus Spoke Zarathustra*, Penguin, UK 1974.
Steiner, Rudolf, *Anthroposophical Leading Thoughts* (CW26), Rudolf Steiner Press, UK 2007.
—, *The Archangel Michael: His Mission and Ours*, Anthroposophic Press, USA 1994.
—, *Awake! For the Sake of the Future* (CW220), Steiner Books, USA 2015.
—, *Karmic Relationships*, Vol. 3 (CW237), Rudolf Steiner Press, UK 1977.
—, *Man in the Light of Occultism, Theosophy and Philosophy* (CW137), Garber Communications, USA 1989.

For news on all our **latest books**,
and to receive **exclusive discounts**,
join our mailing list at:

florisbooks.co.uk/signup

Plus subscribers get a FREE book
with every online order!

We will never pass your details to anyone else.

www.ingramcontent.com/pod-product-compliance
Ingram Content Group UK Ltd.
Pitfield, Milton Keynes, MK11 3LW, UK
UKHW022144090226
467869UK00009B/240